CRISIS COMMUNICATIONS MANAGEMENT

PRCA PRACTICE GUIDES

CRISIS COMMUNICATIONS MANAGEMENT

BY

ADRIAN WHEELER
FPRCA

The Public Relations and Communications Association, UK

United Kingdom — North America — Japan
India — Malaysia — China

Emerald Publishing Limited
Howard House, Wagon Lane, Bingley BD16 1WA, UK

First edition 2019

Reprints and permissions service
Contact: permissions@emeraldinsight.com

British Library Cataloguing in Publication Data
A catalogue record for this book is available from the British Library

ISBN: 978-1-78756-618-7 (Print)
ISBN: 978-1-78756-615-6 (Online)
ISBN: 978-1-78756-617-0 (Epub)

CONTENTS

LIST OF FIGURES

FOREWORD

PRCA Practice Guides are a series of uniquely practical and readable guides, providing PR and communications' professionals, new and experienced alike, with hands-on guidance to manage in the field. Written by experienced practitioners who have been there and done it, the books in the series offer powerful insights into the challenges of the modern industry and guidance on how to navigate your way through them.

This book aims to help PR and communications' practitioners prepare for potential crises, to develop a crisis communications strategy and policy for each client, to take steps to be ready and well-prepared, and to handle communication with media and other stakeholders in a calm and professional manner when a crisis occurs. The book is intended to be a practical guide, so there are numerous examples, checklists and 'what would we have done?' questions scattered throughout the text.

Adrian Wheeler started out as a local newspaper reporter before training at a financial PR firm in the City. He co-founded Sterling Public Relations, a general practice agency, in 1976. This firm became the UK office of GCI Europe. As CEO of GCI UK, Wheeler led the company into the UK Top Ten and in 2000, as chairman of GCI Europe, oversaw the development of a 28-office network with 53 multi-country clients. Since 2006 he has been a partner in Agincourt Communications and a non-executive director at Liquid,

London Communications Agency, and Best Communications in Prague. He is a Fellow of the PRCA and a PR trainer who teaches clients and consultancies throughout Europe and the Middle East.

Francis Ingham
Director General, PRCA
Chief Executive, ICCO

ACKNOWLEDGEMENTS

I would like to thank the many colleagues and friends who have contributed their ideas and experience to the content of this book. Their names are given in the text. I would also like to express my gratitude to Sir Derek Myers, who kindly read the manuscript and pointed out a number of errors and omissions. Those that remain are, of course, my own responsibility.

INTRODUCTION

This book is meant to help PR people advise their clients or employers on doing and saying the right thing in the heat of a crisis.

If your spokesperson comes across as a normal, likeable person who cares, seems to be in control, and speaks like a human being, your organisation or brand will usually survive a crisis unscathed.

If not, you will experience reputational damage. This means reduced sales, eroded margins, a wobbly share price, an impaired licence to operate, employee morale at a low ebb, an inability to attract the best recruits, stakeholder antipathy and aversion from business partners and suppliers.

A poorly handled crisis costs a company money.

Crisis communications management is not a 'nice to have' option. It's about protecting reputational assets, which are an organisation's most valuable possessions.

As PR people, our job is to persuade management that crisis preparation deserves time, money and effort. This can be difficult; managers often believe that 'it will never happen' or that 'we can handle it – don't worry'. This book offers some arguments which can help you to demonstrate reality.

Next, we have to put plans in place. This can be complicated; we may have numerous brands, many sites and a large number of contingencies to consider. What is a reasonable level of investment in crisis communications preparation? This book will help you decide.

Third, when a crisis strikes we need to act quickly and correctly. It can be nerve-wracking. The key decisions are ours and ours alone. This book will help you make the right judgements when everything seems to be spinning out of control.

The author and contributors hope that this book will help you anticipate crises with confidence and with the right systems and materials in place. It is a book, but – as with all PRCA Training products – you are invited to question the author at any time, on any subject connected with crisis communications. The author's Q&A address is given in the Appendix.

No one welcomes a crisis. On the other hand, a well-managed crisis can, paradoxically, enhance a company's reputation. It also proves to our clients and employers that professional public relations is key to what matters to them most: sales, margin, share price, productivity, stakeholder support and *favourability* in the eyes of the outside world.

CHAPTER 1

WHAT *IS* A CRISIS?

The Mail calls to ask about your CFO's private life. A snarky tweet appears saying that your advertising plagiarises a competitor's. The branch manager in Swansea rings to tell you that a customer has slipped on a wet floor and broken her pelvis. The FCA informs the media that your broker is being investigated. An MP puts down a question attacking your relationship with HMRC. The FSA condemns a key ingredient of your major brand.

How do we decide that an event is a *crisis*? Could it instead be an *issue* – which we need to monitor – or is it just a *problem*, the kind of thing managers deal with day in and day out?

It's a judgement call. And it's yours alone, because no one else in the organisation is either qualified or temperamentally suited to say: 'This is the real thing: put the crisis communications machinery into action'.

1.1. ONLY YOU CAN DECIDE

Managers typically downplay crises until it's too late. Then all we are left with is damage limitation. This is understandable: managers are paid to be optimistic and are assumed to be able to predict and control; a nasty surprise isn't part of their natural planning apparatus.

Reactions to crises are subjective. Organisations who are used to everything going like clockwork see any blip as a crisis. At the other end of the spectrum, super-confident managers will think that there is nothing they can't solve with native talent. Both attitudes are likely to be wrong.

That's why your role as an objective expert is crucial. Only you can weigh up the situation without panicking and without false optimism. Only you will appreciate the need for speed.

Unfortunately, in a crisis, we don't have time to be wrong.

Ivy Lee: Game-changer in Crisis Communications

In the late 1800s and the early twentieth century, US railroads were the 'dot.com boom' of the era. Huge fortunes were made by rail monopolists and their investors. The competition was fierce, and slightly mad: lines were built, at massive cost, a few miles away from each other.

Safety standards slipped and crashes were common.

The Pennsylvania Railroad experienced a terrible accident in the town of Gap. The directors invoked the usual SOPs: create an exclusion zone round the crash-site until public interest dwindled.

Ivy Lee, one of the founders of modern PR, was a consultant to the Pennsylvania Railroad. He said: 'No. We will *not* keep the press away. We will do the opposite: we will

> invite them to inspect the site of the crash, tell them why it happened and explain how we will make sure it cannot ever happen again'.
>
> He was a persuasive man. The directors followed his advice and got the best press coverage in the industry that year. They never looked back.
>
> It was Ivy Lee who laid the foundations of present-day crisis communications in 1906. (Museum of Public Relations, 2015.)

1.2. STAKEHOLDERS' OPINIONS MATTER

The idea of *accountability* only took root in the mid-1990s. John Elkington started it with his triad: 'People, Profit, Planet' (*The Economist*, 2009). Before then, most companies felt a duty to communicate with their investors but everything else was either marketing or, as GE called HR, 'the picnic department' (*Financial Post*, 2015).

Anyone reading this book will automatically think in terms of *stakeholders*, but many of our clients don't and others don't want to. It is stakeholder opinion – or, more exactly, sentiment – which controls an organisation's 'licence to operate'. If stakeholders know us and like us, we are well-placed to emerge from a crisis unscathed. If our 'licence to operate' is impaired, we will have trouble.

Business leaders like Lord Browne, Sir Richard Branson and Sir Paul Polman know this instinctively. Others need convincing that stakeholders really matter. We must persuade them that doing and saying the right thing in a crisis is not a choice – it's the *only* way we can protect our reputation when our 'licence to operate' is under threat.

1.3. THE MOST VALUABLE ASSET

Fifty years ago a company's value (its market cap) was mainly measured by objects it owned: plant, inventory, patents, buildings, vehicles and so on – things that could be touched and counted. Today the typical Fortune 500 company's market cap is mostly *intangibles* – brands, popularity, credibility, the CEO's personal profile, goodwill and reputation.

Warren Buffett was the first to say that reputation takes 20 years to build and can vanish overnight. He also told managers at Salomon that he would forgive financial mistakes but would be ruthless if anyone's actions damaged the bank's reputation. Buffett is the ultimate hard-headed investor: what he meant is that *reputation* has a financial value far above anything that can be expressed in a profit & Loss (P&L) (*Forbes*, 2014).

This is why good crisis communications should matter to anyone at the helm of an organisation, whether it's a public company, a public body or a member of the third sector. It's about preserving (or losing) *financial* assets in the form of reputation.

Sir Martin Sorrell made the same point speaking about CSR: 'Some companies see CSR as the icing on the cake. It isn't: doing good is good business' (INSEAD, 2010).

1.4. THE CEO'S PERFORMANCE IS ALL-IMPORTANT

Most of us make snap judgements most of the time. We have to; the average Western European adult is deluged with 4,000 commercial and political messages every day. We rarely think hard or deeply about subjects which don't directly concern ourselves and our families.

As stakeholders, we form a view quickly on whether a company deserves our support and sympathy or whether it deserves to crash and burn. Most of us liked Lord Browne at Beyond Petroleum (BP). We may not have approved of extractive industries, but we liked what Browne said and how he said it. We may even have supported his idea of 'Beyond Petroleum'. But most of us didn't like the way Tony Hayward spoke and behaved in the aftermath of Deepwater Horizon. The consequences for BP's 'licence to operate' have been severe.

Many people (and media) look askance at Sir Richard Branson. Virgin's 'licence to operate' is mixed. But his behaviour and communications when the Virgin Galactic prototype crashed in the Mojave, killing a pilot, were beyond criticism. He got himself to the site as fast as he could. He used Twitter to tell people what he was doing. Once there, he faced the media in person and said the right things. Many people thought differently about Branson, and Virgin, afterwards.

How to Do It Perfectly: James Burke and Tylenol

In 1982 a disaster hit Johnson & Johnson (J&J), one of America's most successful pharmaceutical companies. Tylenol was the country's best-selling analgesic with a 30 per cent market share. It was a major contributor to J&J's P&L.

A maniac (never apprehended) injected Tylenol with cyanide in Chicago pharmacies. Seven people died before the authorities could figure out what was happening.

James Burke, J&J's CEO, was advised to wait and see how things panned out. He said: 'No. we are not going to do that. *We are J&J*. We are going to get back every single tablet of Tylenol from the North American continent.'

He was told this was impossible; no recall expects to recover more than 60 per cent of a faulty product. But Burke was implacable. He went on TV, in person, 24 × 7 and coast-to-coast. His message was simple: if you have Tylenol in your home, do not use it. Take it back to the pharmacy, where you will receive a full refund. DO NOT USE TYLENOL.

It worked. No one else died.

Market-watchers thought this would destroy J&J. They were wrong. The share price wobbled but then held steady for a whole year while Tylenol was off the market.

Investors had decided that Burke was on top of this nightmare. He would sort it out. They trusted him because of his honesty. They admired his bravery.

So did the government. Burke was awarded the Presidential Medal of Freedom in 2000 for putting the interests of the American public before those of his company.

(*International Herald Tribune*, 2002)

How to Do It Perfectly: Michael Bishop and the Kegworth Crash

Michael Bishop started work in airlines when he was 16. He eventually got the chance to set up his own: British Midland (BM), a short-haul carrier which became very popular with business travellers. BM went from strength to strength.

Then something terrible happened. A 737 came in to land at Kegworth (Peterborough) when an engine flamed out.

Unfortunately, the pilot switched off the other engine, so the aircraft crashed on the airfield boundary and 47 people were killed.

Bishop was called by his PA, who lived nearby. 'Michael – you should get here quickly – I have heard a dreadful noise at the airfield.' He jumped into his car, unshaven and wearing a cardigan. On the way, the media started calling his mobile phone. 'What's happened?'

Of course, he didn't know. We *never* know the details when a crisis strikes.

But he *did* know what to say. He spoke from the heart, unabashed. 'These are *my* passengers. These are *my* crew – they are all friends of mine'.

When he got to Kegworth he insisted on facing the cameras and mics alone. It was *his* airline. For a week, as the top news item, Bishop couldn't say *why* the crash had happened. But he could say how he felt about it and what BM was doing to help the victims' relatives and the survivors.

Everyone thought that BM was finished. Not so. Ticket-sales rose and the company grew strongly until it was eventually bought by BA.

What was happening here? Michael Bishop's sheer honesty and likeability overcame all other considerations. We admired him. We trusted him. We believed he would look after us.

Bishop was knighted two years later.

(Media First, 2014)

1.5. CRISIS COMMUNICATIONS

There's a lot of information and advice in this book. We hope readers will be able to make use of much of it. But it's obvious that many organisations don't have the resources to put a full-fledged crisis communication plan in place and keep it up to date.

For these PR professionals, our advice is this: *the CEO's performance is critical.*

Your organisation, company or brand will be judged by how well (or poorly) the CEO behaves in the glare of media attention.

If your crisis communications plans are rudimentary, but your CEO performs well, you will – with any luck – survive the crisis with your 'licence to operate' intact.

If your plans are near-perfect but your CEO wavers, hides, does the wrong thing, says the wrong thing – or simply does and says *nothing* – you will probably suffer reputational injury.

If you haven't the money or the time to do anything else, get the CEO on-board and trained to handle media and stakeholder communications properly in crisis conditions.

1.6. WHAT IS A CRISIS, THEN?

Are people's lives, health or welfare at risk?

Does the organisation need to *act* to protect anyone's lives, health or welfare – whether or not the event is its own responsibility?

Could media scrutiny portray the organisation – fairly or unfairly – in a way which will lose approval from stakeholders?

How would the most admired organisation in our sector react in these circumstances?

If we were stakeholders (for instance, employees, customers and retailers), what response would make us feel proud of the organisation?

As the organisation's PR department or consultancy, what kind of response would make us feel we had stepped up to the plate in a moral, professional and brave manner?

Crises test the character of organisations in a way that nothing else does. The temptation is always to duck, delay and hope it all blows over. This may have worked years ago, but it doesn't work now.

Experience shows that it is better to treat an unwelcome event as a crisis, even if it turns out not to be, than to hope it won't be, when it is.

A Good Example: Admiral Cunningham

The British invaded Greece in 1941. It was not a good idea; they were chased out by the Wehrmacht and took up positions in Crete, hoping to turn it into an island fortress. That didn't work, either; the Germans landed on Crete with gliders and parachutists. The British had to be evacuated, and the task – once again – fell to the Royal Navy.

The evacuation was a success, but not for the Royal Navy. An aircraft carrier, three cruisers and five destroyers were all sunk by the *Luftwaffe* with the loss of 2,600 sailors' lives.

At the height of the mayhem one of Admiral Cunningham's officers asked him if it was worth it.

Without hesitation, Cunningham turned to this officer and said: 'It takes the Royal Navy three years to build a ship.

It has taken us 300 years to build our reputation. We must *not* let these men down.'

This is a classic example of the person in charge of both *doing* and *saying* the right thing in the midst of a real life-and-death crisis.

(HistoryNet, 2007)

Summary

What *Is* a Crisis?

Is it a problem, an issue or a genuine crisis?

As a rule, the decision is yours, advising the CEO.

Are people's lives, health or welfare at risk? If so, it's probably a crisis.

Reputation is a financial asset. If it's in jeopardy, serious money is at stake.

By definition, a crisis is a surprise. ANY level of planning will help us handle it.

The spokesperson's performance is critical.

The spokesperson must be the CEO.

CHAPTER 2

PERSUADING MANAGEMENT TO PREPARE

A crisis is a manager's worst nightmare, but it can be difficult to persuade management to put even basic preparations in place.

Sometimes the reasons are practical. Budgets are stretched ... the communications team is under-strength ... PR is seen as part of marketing and has no corporate function ...

Just as often, the reasons are emotional. 'It'll never happen to *us*!' 'We can handle it ...' 'Look at the problems Facebook are having! It doesn't seem to have done them any harm!'

Without preparation, a crisis will definitely be an unpleasant experience that damages managers' confidence and can cause lasting damage to brands and corporate reputation.

With preparation, a crisis can usually be survived and can even – paradoxically – enhance an organisation's reputational assets.

2.1. IT'S ALL ABOUT THE CEO

The days are long gone when a young executive from a company's lawyers could read out a crisis statement in front of the cameras, mics and reporters.

Today, the media expect the CEO to act as the face and voice of a company in trouble. Nothing less is acceptable. The absence of the CEO is automatically presumed to mean guilt.

This makes crisis preparation even more difficult for us. It's not just a corporate communications function: it directly and personally involves the most senior person in the organisation – someone we may not meet from one month to the next.

But that's how it is.

Everything a CEO cares about is thrown into jeopardy by poor crisis communications, including his or her own job.

2.2. SHARE PRICE AND MARKET CAP

For public companies the consequences of *mis-managing* crisis communications are serious. Oxford Metrica's records show that in most cases it's not the details of a crisis that do the damage – it's almost always how investors and other stakeholders *perceive* the company's behaviour in the media spotlight. Impressions count. Facts – often in short supply – are less important.

The CEO's performance makes all the difference.

This makes sense. Human beings are not very good at assembling information and making rational decisions. They are very good indeed at making judgements about other people.

Gurus from Dale Carnegie to Nobel Prize winner Daniel Kahneman have explained why. We make snap judgements based on sketchy impressions from our eyes and ears.

Eighty per cent of the impact of a speech or presentation comes not from *what* was said but by *how* it was said, and *how* the speaker behaved.

To protect the share price, the CEO must be front and central in a crisis, doing and saying the right thing. James Burke of J&J and Michael Bishop of BM are good examples. Sir Richard Branson has the courage to face up to Virgin's problems in person. When Dara Khosrowshahi took over as CEO of Uber in 2017, he impressed the media by speaking frequently and frankly about the company's problems.

2.3. 'IT'LL NEVER HAPPEN TO US'

But it probably will.

In 2000, companies faced a two-to-one chance that they would experience a crisis in a five-year period. By 2010, the odds had shortened to four to one.

The Internet, and in particular social media, have a lot to do with this. So does the growing idea of *accountability*: consumer activists and active consumers.

So does the increasing media power of Non-Governmental Organisations (NGOs) and Single-Interest Group (SIGs). So does the prevalence of whistle-blowers, granted legal protection and rewards in many Organisation for Economic Co-Operation and Development (OECD) countries.

Companies make mistakes. Sometimes these have lethal consequences. Sometimes the effects, if not the motives, receive public condemnation. Nowadays, a small mis-step can have disproportionate reputational results.

It's no longer 'if' but 'when'.

2.4. BE PREPARED

This book will talk about the levels of preparation which may be appropriate for the organisation you work for or represent. What is certain is that *no* preparation is always wrong.

But all your work will be pointless if the CEO is not equipped to step up to the plate and act as the company's spokesperson in the event of a crisis.

He or she has to be ready to drop everything else and focus on the key task of representing the organisation in public, under duress. He or she will usually be feeling isolated: the chairman and other board members often keep to the sidelines.

Your role is to give the CEO all the support he or she needs to perform creditably.

The 'Titanic Effect'

Schlosser (2013), in his book, *Command and Control*, states: 'The more impossible an accident is believed to be, the more likely it becomes'.

Illusions

The book *World Order* (Kissinger, 2014) states: 'Paradoxically, success in resolving crises can breed a form of risk-taking unmoored from reality'.

Tiger Woods

The University of California, Davis, calculated that *US$12 billion* was wiped off the market-cap of Tiger Woods' corporate sponsors in the wake of his 'marital problems' (Reuters Staff, 2009).

Donnelly's Principle

'Companies that handle crises well ... you never hear about them'.

James Donnelly, Senior Vice President at Ketchum

Whose engine blew up on a Qantas A380, the airline's first-ever serious incident?

Who made the reactor containment vessel which failed at Fukushima?

Crisis preparation is an *investment*

'Every $1 invested in crisis management returns $7 in averted costs'

Marsh Consulting

Summary

Persuading Management to Prepare

Managers are often reluctant to invest time and money in preparation.

They face a four-to-one risk of a crisis in any five-year period.

A dollar invested in crisis management returns US$7 in averted costs.

Good communications enhance reputational assets in a crisis.

Communications matter more than the details of the crisis itself.

No hiding-place. Delay and confusion are interpreted as guilt.

In a crisis, preparation is everything.

CHAPTER 3

STRATEGY: PRINCIPLES OF CRISIS COMMUNICATIONS

You are thinking about your crisis communications plan. What shape and size should it be? Most of us aim to come up with a set of processes, systems and materials which will help us handle a crisis but without going overboard. How can we decide what level of preparation is proportionate?

There isn't a formula and there isn't a textbook. But here are some *principles* which, we hope, will help you decide how much time, money and effort you should invest in crisis communications preparation.

3.1. PREPARATION IS EVERYTHING

The option of doing nothing and saying nothing is *not an option*. In a crisis, we must be ready to step forward and speak out. If we fail to do this, or if we do it unconvincingly, the consequences are likely to be severe. As far as the media are concerned, silence and confusion imply guilt.

This means that however large or small our organisation is, however centralised or dispersed, whether we are in B2C or B2B and whether we have a proficient or a rudimentary communications team, some level of crisis communications preparation is essential.

Get Outside Advice

Remember the last time you watched – through the eyes and ears of the media – a crisis developing, like a slow-motion car crash? Or, perhaps more accurately, a motorway pile-up. That initial mistake leading to further collisions with other vehicles (the media, government, angry campaign groups and so on) until a vast disaster forms.

What is the striking similarity between the companies at the centre of so many of these crises? They all appear to be incapable of taking advice from outside their organisations.

Like a traumatised individual going dead in the eyes and adopting the brace position, the crisis-hit company will often shut down and rely on anodyne legal statements. It's the death-knell for any organisation aiming to weather the storm... the media smell *fear*.

My advice may seem obvious, but it's often overlooked.

Bring in a consultancy or a freelancer who can, at the very least, act as a sounding-board for your messages. Talk to contacts, both inside and outside your own industry. Try mentors and friends whose intelligence you respect.

Let your guard down, open up, talk about your hopes and worries. Build a rounded view by discussing one advisor's suggestions with another. You'll feel yourself learning.

> We can't expect every business leader to be an expert on crisis handling. But they do have a responsibility to know when the time has come to take advice on board. Because what's the alternative? Hubris.
>
> *Matt Cartmell has worked in PR consultancy and as a member of the UK* PRWeek *editorial team. He is now Deputy Director General at the PRCA.*

3.2. WE HAVE NO IDEA WHAT MIGHT HAPPEN!

Of course not. However, experience shows that even the most basic attention to crisis communications planning will be valuable when the worst comes to the worst. Thinking about contingencies and stakeholders, preparing materials, getting spokespeople media-trained … we may feel we have not done enough, and it's probably true – but we are nevertheless creating a kind of 'muscle memory' which will help us and our colleagues react constructively when we get *that call* or spot *that post.*

3.3. COMMUNICATIONS ARE MORE IMPORTANT THAN THE DETAILS OF THE CRISIS

If you are reading this book, you already know that stakeholders are strongly influenced by perception and less so by facts. Audiences will usually form their view of a troubled company by the way its senior people appear on TV, on the radio and in the mainstream and online media. Are they sincere, human, in control? That's normally enough for most stakeholders.

Key Crisis Questions

A real crisis is when someone is wronged, hurt or even killed. When a crisis happens you need to answer the *key crisis questions* as soon as possible.

What happened?

Why did it happen?

What are you going to do about it now?

What will you do to ensure it doesn't happen again?

Are you sorry? The answer is always 'yes' even if the crisis wasn't directly your fault. As a minimum, you are sorry for others' misfortune.

Any delay in telling the truth, helping the victims and saying sorry turns a disaster into a 'PR disaster'. A PR disaster happens when an organisation's behaviour and communication cause people to lose respect, trust and liking for it. The damage from a PR disaster usually lasts far longer than the damage from the original crisis.

Trevor Morris is the former CEO of Chime Public Relations, Professor of Communications at Richmond University and the author of several books including 'PR for the New Europe'. *He is a member of the PRCA Training faculty.*

Professional communicators know this but managers tend to believe that *the facts speak for themselves* … we need to convince our spokespeople, early in the planning process, that their 'performance' will be critical to survival in a crisis. This often goes against the grain.

Communications Might *Not* Be the Solution

Crisis communications isn't a magic wand. Sometimes a company's problems are so self-inflicted or endemic that the only real answer is a root-and-branch re-boot.

Here is Dara Khosrowshahi when he took over from Travis Kalanick at Uber: 'It's critical that we act with integrity in everything we do... building trust through our actions and behaviour'.

Mr Khosrowshahi's instincts were spot-on. By talking about the behavioural problems at Uber rather than the company's atrocious media profile, he won his employees' trust and his stakeholders' respect (Statt, 2017).

3.4. THERE IS NO HIDING-PLACE

Professional communicators know that we live in the media spotlight 24 × 7 × 52. It's what Paul Johnson called 'the modern electronic democracy'. He went on to say: 'When the media fill a large part of our lives... the PR people have to be present at the policy-making stage, when the actions are decided' (*The Spectator*, 1984). If you are the CEO of United Airlines, you will have to answer for the behaviour of airport security personnel (not your employees) within hours, and you will have to get it right. It can be a frightening challenge.

Many CEOs – perhaps most – would prefer things to be different. They would like time to take advice, consult, reach a consensus and then – maybe – issue a statement.

The world isn't like that any more. There is no hiding-place and there is precious little time to decide what to say and then say it. We have to convince our spokespeople that they will need to react fast and get it right. With our help.

Being Human Beats Being Right

I can offer three pieces of advice about handling a crisis effectively.

One: always put people first. Most of us are forgiving if an organisation responds with humanity. It's essential that every person impacted by the crisis – employees, customers, the community, families and so on – is very clearly treated as the Number One Priority.

Two: it's important that the main spokesperson is someone local – not someone 'parachuted in' from HQ. The local person has local context; they can speak as a human being. You will need other spokespeople to draw on, including the CEO – but make the lead someone local.

Third: in a crisis, it's not about *being right* but about *doing the right thing*. There are many examples of organisations which focus on winning the argument rather than handling the crisis well. They suffer lasting reputational damage.

Take advice from your experts – and from your lawyers – but don't let them prevent you from behaving and speaking like a human being.

Crispin Manners is a former PRCA chairman and the CEO of Onva Consulting.

3.5. A SMALL 'CRISIS' CAN RAPIDLY ESCALATE

Something happens. A media call, a YouTube clip, maybe a question in the House. Is this a crisis? Should we put the machinery in motion? Or should we wait and see what happens next?

This is the key decision. It's a judgement call. It's *your* call, because only you – as a professional communicator – have the experience and objectivity to say *go* or *wait*.

In my own experience, it's better to say *go* – and then be criticised because nothing actually happened – than to say *wait and see*. It's tricky: we must avoid crying wolf.

It's better for our organisation to gear up than to be caught napping.

3.6. 'DO WE HAVE TO SAY *ANYTHING?*'

I have heard this 100 times. You have probably heard it too. Managers obviously prefer to remain silent when they don't have the facts to hand. It's understandable; managers succeed by being sure of the information they impart. Most managers are not natural or trained communicators. They are comfortable with the 'hard' disciplines rather than the 'soft' arts of communication, public speaking and stakeholder engagement. Few CEOs come from sales.

In a crisis, our spokespeople are required to display skills which they may not naturally possess. It's unfair, to say the least, to expose them to media scrutiny without training, rehearsal and guidance. Yes, in a crisis we *do* have to say something. It must be the right thing, and we have to say it in a way that evokes sympathy and support.

Truth and Lies

'A lie can travel half-way round the world while the truth is putting on its shoes'. So said nineteenth century English Particular Baptist preacher Charles Spurgeon (don't ask).

Spurgeon was in PR, of sorts. As I once was – though secular. I write with the benefit of hindsight; it's 15 years since I did PR myself and those years – working alongside PR consultants in crisis situations – have taught me that I had something right all along, even if I wasn't thanked for it at the time.

What was right was *truth*. Twenty years ago a hotel client suffered an outbreak of legionella. A guest died. The client panicked. We dispatched a senior colleague to take control. Her mantra was: Never *no comment*. Truth always. Don't hide behind walls or gates. Never fear saying sorry.

All of which she kept to – and all of which the client argued against. To my surprise the client's lawyers agreed with the senior colleague. Long story short: the problem was contained, environmental health and HSE were on-side, remedial action was taken and the coverage ground to a halt.

The death was a needless tragedy. Lack of oversight had allowed the infection to breed. In terms of 'PR' it was as good as it could be. It is only acts of nature that are not, somewhere, triggered or exacerbated by human error (and sometimes malice or stupidity). The lesson is, I think, that the more defensive your client is, the more likely it is that there is a cock-up somewhere.

Years later I watched as a PR firm I was working alongside mis-managed a different death. Meaningless holding statements, nothing on the website, management in a cupboard, an attempted distraction ('it's happened worse to others'), a counter-attack (blame someone else) and no one facing the cameras. That story still crops up.

In a crisis, the truth is by far your best weapon.

Christopher Broadbent founded Barclay Stratton. For the last 10 years he has been a sustainability consultant.

3.7. STRONG LEADERSHIP IS ESSENTIAL

An organisation in a crisis is a sad thing. It reacts with panic and paralysis. No one knows what's happening ... events are moving fast, out of control ... outside scrutiny is intense ... the media speculate and managers get angry ... a siege mentality sets in, with a short-term focus ... management freezes ... normal business is forgotten ... the organisation *looks* bad and *feels* bad.

What's needed is *strong leadership*. We want Attila the Hun. For most senior managers these days, this is an unusual way to behave: the fashion is for managers to be guides, coaches ... supportive ... encouraging their employees to give of their best, which means meetings, discussion, consultation and consensus. Of course, this works ... except in a crisis.

There is no time to ask what everyone thinks. Someone – the CEO – has to make on-the-spot decisions, himself or herself. Their only advisor should be their communications professional.

Unless our CEO or client is a natural autocrat, *we* are responsible for giving them a preview of what a crisis is actually like. No consultations or consensus... rapid, personal decisions, followed by personal statements, delivered in person.

For this, crisis simulations are worth their weight in gold.

Tim Traverse-Healy's Unusual PR Role

Tim Traverse-Healy was a founder of the UK PR industry. One of his first clients was a bank which eventually became part of NatWest, and then RBS.

Traverse-Healy was an impressive man: tall, strong, an ex-Commando and a practising Roman Catholic.

> His job was to attend the bank's board meetings and listen to what they were saying. Every so often he had to bang his fist on the table: 'You can't do that!' he would roar.
>
> The frightened bankers would ask 'why?'
>
> 'Because you are ripping off your customers! You are taking advantage of the trust they place in you! This is immoral, unconscionable. It's wrong!'
>
> The bank would meekly change its plans.

3.8. REMEMBER THIRD PARTIES

The media are the most obvious stakeholder group in a crisis. Most crises are either triggered by media attention or fuelled by media interest.

Our other stakeholder groups, whether individuals or categories, are equally important. Not only are they Key Opinion Formers (KOFs) in their own right, but they are often consulted by the media when journalists are trying to decide whether to write the story up, down or flat.

The 'top tip' regarding other stakeholders is to tell them, personally, whatever we are telling the media, at the same time.

This means owning stakeholder databases or having quick access to them. With GDPR it also means, as a rule of thumb, having permission to communicate with stakeholders proactively.

3.9. CRISIS PREPARATION IS AN *INVESTMENT*

If it's going to work, crisis preparation is a board-level decision. The CEO must be personally committed and available. He or she must be trained and ready to do the job properly.

We may meet opposition from the financial director. 'Is it really worth devoting all this money to something that may never happen?'

It's a fair question from someone who will never have to face the media in a crisis. It may help us to present crisis communications preparation as a form of insurance, a bit like PI. It's an *investment in crisis readiness*.

We can quote Marsh Consulting: 'Every dollar invested in crisis management returns seven dollars in averted costs'.

3.10. THE 'GOLDEN HOUR'

We have *one hour* from the moment we know about a crisis until we issue our initial statement.

It is sometimes said that, in an age of social media, we must react in minutes.

Not true.

We *need* an hour to verify the threat, decide how best to handle it and – if it is judged to be a potential crisis – compose our initial response and how to disseminate it.

We must get it right first time.

3.11. SEIZE THE MEDIA INITIATIVE AND KEEP IT

The media expect organisations in crisis to hide, delay, obfuscate and remain silent. This tempts them to behave, in Tony Blair's words, as 'feral beasts' (Alan, 2007).

Instead, we should set our own media timetable and stick to it. This means issuing our initial statement (in person, onsite ... and via all our other channels) and then telling the media that our next up-date will be in an hour ... two hours ....

At the stated time, our spokesperson comes back to the steps/the podium/the crash-site and gives the next bulletin. There may be nothing new to report.

Then he or she tells the media that the next up-date will be delivered in an hour … two hours ….

This has two good effects. It tells the media that we are *not* hiding but are, instead, trying to help them do their job – reporting on the crisis. Second, it relieves some of the pressure on our communications team: if journalists believe we will keep them up-to-date voluntarily, they will be less inclined to deluge our team with calls and emails.

3.12. LOOKING AHEAD

Sir Derek Myers points out that most crises encourage a short-term focus. What are the media saying *now*? What should we say *now*? Someone needs to be looking ahead.

If it's *not* our own crisis, but in the same sector, will the media look for son-and-daughter or brother-and-sister stories? Could we be in the firing-line?

If it's our crisis and it escalates, *who* might say *what* and how should we respond? Will the government comment? It often does. Will there be an enquiry? There often is, and our spokesperson may be called to give evidence. Will there be a Select Committee hearing? If so, our spokesperson will need further training and rehearsal: these grillings are not pleasant.

Will our CEO resign? If so, what is the right tone for his or her successor to adopt?

3.13. THE CEO MUST BE THE CENTRAL FIGURE

The media expect and demand that the boss – the CEO – will be the person who tells them what's happening in a

crisis. They expect the CEO to step up and take personal responsibility.

It was not always so. But today it is. The media will accept nothing less. Woe betide a CEO in the twenty-first century who hopes to hide behind a 'spokesperson'. It happens, but it's a very unwise strategy.

This means that our CEO must be properly trained and ready to face the media in a crisis. A tall order in many organisations, but it's our responsibility – as professional communicators – to equip our employer or client to handle a crisis in accordance with best practice.

In a Crisis, the CEO Is a Lonely Person

To paraphrase Eric Dezenhall, a highly-rated Washington corporate strategist, '*A corporation in a crisis isn't a corporation. It's a collection of panicked individuals motivated by self-preservation.*'

(*Washington Post*, 2008)

Cynical, but true.

The CEO, whose face and voice are the emblems of the crisis, is usually very lonely. Her or his career is on the line. In a crisis, a CEO only has one absolutely loyal friend. You.

Survive the crisis together and you very often forge a bond for life.

3.14. LOG AND LEARN

Who has time to keep records in the maelstrom of a crisis? Probably not many of us. But it pays dividends. Keep notes. Who asked what, what was said in reply. What coverage resulted. What our spokesperson said and how it was treated by the media. How our stakeholders reacted to the information we issued. Some organisations dump everything on a wiki for later analysis. The key is to make sure every interaction with the media and other stakeholders is captured.

Is it worth it? Yes.

All crisis communications programmes are, to some extent, experimental. We want to figure out what worked and what didn't, so that we can do better next time.

3.15. CALM, COOL, CAPABLE, CAREFUL AND COLLECTED

We may have 50 people in our communications team or just two. They may be in a single office or scattered around the world. All of them are in the front line when a crisis hits.

The media are at their worst when they are reporting a crisis; they are under pressure and they very often transfer that pressure to the team. They can be aggressive, provocative, insistent, demanding and downright rude.

It takes nerve, professionalism and character to continue to give a good service when the media are behaving like this, especially when a crisis lasts for days or weeks.

Give the team crisis communications training. Let them experience (simulated) media onslaughts at their most aggressive.

The media normally make judgements about an organisation according to the service (or lack of it) that they receive from the media relations team – which is usually their only point of contact. If they feel they are well-treated by the media relations team, they will feel less-inclined to be hostile to the organisation they work for or represent.

Summary

Strategy: Principles of Crisis Communications

A small crisis can rapidly escalate.

'Do we have to say anything?' Yes.

No time for consensus. Strong leadership is essential.

It's not just about the media. Inform stakeholders and third parties.

We have an hour – 'The Golden Hour' – even in an age of social media.

We must seize the media initiative and keep it.

Be calm, capable, concerned, careful and collected; show empathy.

CHAPTER 4

CONTINGENCY PLANNING

What could go wrong? We want to narrow down the possibilities but we should not overlook extremely unlikely events – *perfect storms* – because these can and do happen.

It may be helpful to divide contingencies into three categories.

Catastrophes, calamities and Acts of God: As a rule, we needn't be too concerned with these: if a meteorite falls on our factory or a flood puts it out of action, our duty is to co-operate with the emergency services and look after anyone who has been affected. Our communications have to say this clearly, but we are not normally under duress.

Collateral and peripheral: This could be where a supplier has fallen down with effects on our own ability to deliver proper quality, on time and in a normal manner. It might also be when a sponsored celebrity has misbehaved, with – irrationally – a negative effect on our own reputation. The rule in these circumstances is to vow to put things right with customers – and never, ever shift responsibility onto the supplier (though this is often managers' first reaction).

The third category, which is the topic of this book, is when *fault, negligence or blame* is imputed to our client or employer, either fairly or unfairly. This is when the media's fangs are bared and when our organisation is at risk of serious reputational damage.

4.1. WOW BOX

To plan contingencies, we use a simple Boston Grid with 'probability' as the *x* axis and 'damage' as the *y*. To populate the quadrants, we hold a brainstorm; the more different kinds of people we involve – everyone from engineering to finance to security – the better the results we get.

The brainstorm follows the usual rules: no discussion or debate, all ideas are welcome. Afterwards, we use our judgement to place the contingencies in the quadrants where they belong (Figure 1).

The top-right-hand quadrant is the 'WoW Box' – the Worst of the Worst. These are the contingencies – ideally 8 or 10 – which we will use as the basis for our planning, processes, materials preparation and training.

Circumstances change, so we should review our contingency model every three months.

As an adjunct to the contingency grid we may want to hold a PESTLE brainstorm, where we and our colleagues try to foresee trends or changes which may affect reputational hazards in the coming two or three years: Political, Economic, Societal, Technological, Legal and Environmental.

Figure 1. Reputational Hazards Contingency Planning.

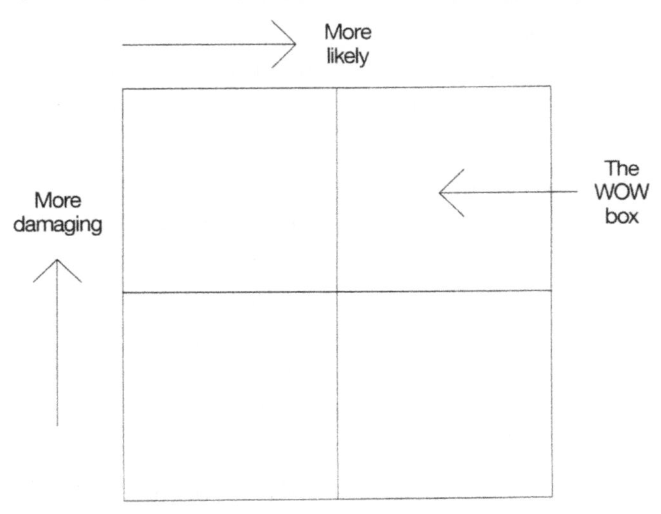

Contingency Planning: Expecting the Unexpected

By 2004 Crocs, an Australian beach sandal, had become a global love-brand with a market cap of $4.5 billion. The company had big plans to expand into other areas of branded apparel.

In 2007, George Bush was photographed wearing crocs. With socks.

By 2013, Crocs' market cap was $0.9 billion.

Bush wasn't the only reason, but he was one of them.

Look at Burberry and how close they came to disaster when they were adopted by 'chavs'.

When you are doing contingency planning, think about possibilities which seem off the map.

Contingency Planning: The Lucretius Problem

Nassim Nicholas Taleb (2012), author of *The Black Swan*, reminds us in *Antifragile* that the 'worst of the worst' may be something many times worse than we can imagine.

He quotes the Roman poet Lucretius, who said that a fool believes that the highest mountain in existence is the one he can see, while a mountain twice as high might be right behind him.

A good example is Fukushima, where the designers – knowing earthquakes are common in the area – made the containment vessel strong enough to resist twice the force of any earthquake in history.

Then, a much stronger earthquake struck and the vessel was overwhelmed.

Moral: think *inside* the boxes when planning contingencies, then think *outside* them.

Contingency Planning: Peripheral Factors

This seems incredible, but it's true: the University of California's Davis campus calculated that Tiger Woods' sponsors lost $12 billion in market cap when his marital problems hit the news.

Why? What possible connection could there be between Tiger Woods' personal issues and the fortunes of corporations which happened to have paid to use his name ... Gatorade, EA, Accenture, Tag Heuer, AT&T, Gillette and so on?

But the damage was done and they all dumped him. Except one.

Do you know which sponsor stuck with Tiger Woods, and why?

Summary

Contingency Planning

Catastrophes, calamities and disasters – 'Acts of God'.

Peripheral or collateral crises; for example, the supply chain and sponsorships.

Blame, negligence and fault – our reputation is at risk.

Brainstorm possibilities using a four-quadrant box.

Use the 'Worst of the Worst' for materials and practice.

The Lucretius Principle – imagine the unimaginable.

Involve spokespeople in contingency planning.

CHAPTER 5

STAKEHOLDER IDENTIFICATION AND LISTS

We need to ascertain whose decisions are crucial and whose opinions are important to us in a crisis, then organise lists – or access to lists – so that we can communicate with them regularly as the crisis unfolds.

Most professional communications teams maintain lists of key decision makers (KDMs) and key opinion formers (KOFs). They have lists of their primary and secondary media contacts.

These are a good start, but when a crisis strikes, we usually want to communicate with larger and wider groups of stakeholders – active, passive and possibly even latent.

Compiling and maintaining crisis-ready stakeholder lists is often the most time-consuming and tricky aspect of crisis preparation.

5.1. 'SEND IT OUT TO THE MEDIA – ISN'T THAT ENOUGH?'

Managers sometimes think our role in PR is to handle the media. This is certainly one of our key functions. But 'public' relations imply a wider responsibility, and this is never more true than in times of crisis.

It's useful – and important – to keep as many of our stakeholders in the picture as we possibly can. We cannot rely on the media alone to present 'our side of the story'. We need to talk to people directly.

A rule of thumb is to tell our stakeholders whatever we are telling the media, at the same time.

Do we have to? Do we need to add yet another level of complexity and cost to our crisis communications machinery?

Yes. When a crisis embroils us, a large number of stakeholders will wonder what's happening and may begin to doubt our stability – they may even wonder if we will survive. An example was the fate of Carillion in January 2018. As rumours and then media coverage of the group's financial problems gathered momentum, banks and suppliers had to decide whether or not to pull the plug. Carillion was unable to present a convincing case and was forced into liquidation, when – in fact – it might have been possible to preserve a huge company and thousands of jobs by driving through the crisis.

5.2. EMPLOYEES – OFTEN NEGLECTED IN A CRISIS

Strangely, employees usually find out that their company is in crisis by watching the TV news.

Nothing could be better designed to dampen their spirits and destroy their morale.

This doesn't make sense. Employees are not only the source of our productivity, they are also our most effective ambassadors to the outside world. Edelman's Trust Barometer shows that company spokespeople command alarmingly low levels of credibility today. But people trust 'people like us'. The local media will take their lead from employees they interview at the factory gate or in the local pub. The local community will believe what their neighbours say.

Employees should be told what's happening and kept regularly updated. The message is that we have a problem and this is how we are dealing with it: candid, confident, upbeat.

5.3. USING THE INFLUENCE/INTEREST GRID

We would like to talk to all our stakeholders simultaneously. Perhaps we have the resources to do so, but probably not. So it's useful to work out, in advance, which stakeholders are our priorities. We can use a standard stakeholder prioritisation tool, the I/I Grid (Figure 2). It's another Boston Box, sometimes called a 'Power Grid'.

An illustration is presented here, and at the back of the book is a stakeholder checklist which may help to ensure that no groups or individuals are overlooked in planning.

We should review our lists every three months.

5.4. WHO OWNS THE LISTS?

This can present a problem. In a crisis, we need instant and perhaps frequent access to databases which in many cases are 'owned' by other departments in the organisation. Employee lists, for instance, are almost always 'owned' by HR.

Figure 2. Stakeholder Prioritisation.

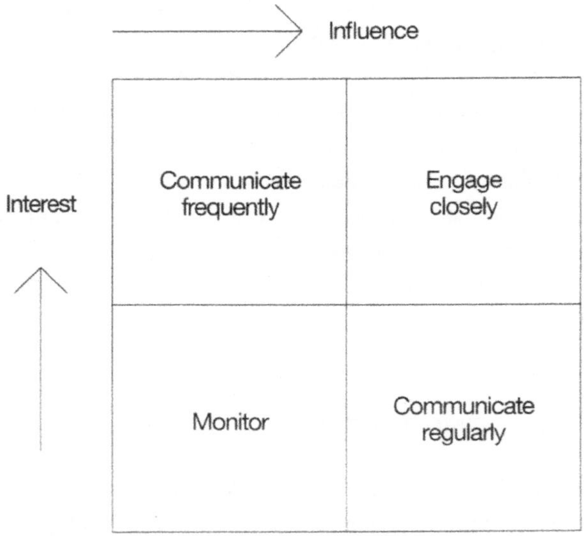

Influence →

Interest ↑

Communicate frequently	Engage closely
Monitor	Communicate regularly

Customer lists may be 'owned' by sales, marketing, support or Customer Relationship Management (CRM). Our Investor Relations (IR) team has the names of people responsible for managing their funds' investment in our equity. Can we access this list in a crisis?

In comms, we have our own lists (compliant, of course, with GDPR) but in a crisis, we need to send our messages *directly* to a much wider range of stakeholders ... possibly people we (in comms) will *only* need to speak to in a crisis.

We need to think about these stakeholder categories and who 'owns' the lists. Will we have access to them in a crisis? If not, what can we do about it in advance?

Summary

Stakeholder Identification and Lists

We should inform stakeholders at the same time as the media.

Employees are often ignored. Why?

Regular updates show we are on top of the crisis.

The 'commentariat' (talking heads) will be asked for opinions.

Prioritise stakeholders using the I/I Grid.

Set up rapid stakeholder communications channels in advance.

Who 'owns' the lists? Can we access them in a crisis?

CHAPTER 6

HOW THE MEDIA DRIVE CRISES

A crisis is a *good story*. Journalists' eyes light up. They become even more competitive than usual. Editors want the story first and best.

Verification can be sidelined in the race to judgement.

Murray Sayle, head of the *Sunday Times* Insight Team, said there were only two stories: '*Arrow points to defective part*' and '*We name the guilty men*' (*The Telegraph*, 2010).

Chris Blackhurst, writing in *The Independent*, explained why the media are often hostile when they report an organisation's troubles:

A recurring post-crash mystery is the collective failure of the banks, with their armies of spin-doctors and reputation advisers, to see how others regard them and do something about it (*The Independent*, 2014).

Jeremy Warner in the *Telegraph* offers another reason: 'When confronting a crisis, executives are too reluctant to accept wrong-doing and too slow to respond... especially in large companies unused to failure of any kind' (*Daily Telegraph*, 2010).

A Journalist's Perspective

The mainstream media tend to view every sort of organisational crisis as a 'PR disaster', whereas I would distinguish between the two. The former is when an organisational mis-step causes negative media coverage; the latter is when an organisation actively mis-handles an issue – or responds unprofessionally to a crisis, thereby exacerbating the reputational damage caused.

Any organisation will make operational errors from time to time, but *crises* only occur when these are of sufficient magnitude: people are hurt or put at risk, customers are massively inconvenienced or the organisation's 'licence to operate' is challenged. But crises can also be self-inflicted, arising from sheer lack of professionalism in dealing with an issue.

The media – always seeking a juicy story – have scant natural sympathy for organisations undergoing difficulty, but they will be much more aggressive if there is little or no communication from the organisation – and that means the boss.

The 'golden rules' for handling a crisis are: (1) to respond quickly. Peter Mandelson advised: 'Don't say anything until you have the facts but don't say nothing for too long – or someone else will fill the void'. (2) the boss – chief executive, minister, director-general – must be visible on the front line.

The boss needs to take responsibility for the problem – quickly – displaying leadership and empathy. Organisational lawyers may advise bosses to avoid accepting liability, but this does not mean absolving themselves of responsibility or failing to show empathy; both are crucial to stop a bad situation getting worse. This requires emotional intelligence from the boss and continuous updating, information and advice from his or her communications advisers.

Within 24 hours, however, the media will be expecting more than empathy. They will be demanding to know how the organisation plans to improve the situation. The crisis plan is now at stage two and there is still a long way to go ... it's important to keep the media in the picture as the recovery strategy unfolds.

Danny Rogers is UK Editor-in-Chief of PR Week *and the author of* Campaigns that Shook the World: the Evolution of Public Relations (2015).

6.1. CAN WE EVER WIN?

CEOs subjected to this kind of animosity sometimes lose heart. 'We can't win!' We can, but it needs strong nerves, knowledge of what the media want and practice in talking to them in the language and manner that they respect.

Journalists are human beings like the rest of us. It is hard for them to go for the jugular if they feel that a CEO is doing his or her best, making an effort to be helpful and behaving like a normal person rather than a robot. This means that our CEO *can* win media approval if they take the initiative and face the music.

Some CEOs do this naturally, but most don't. They will be nervous – their career may be on the line. They will feel isolated. A crisis is a shock; the natural reaction is to hide. When they speak to the media, they often retreat into a wooden mode of expression.

How (Not) to Apologise: Why Tone of Voice Is Everything

You might call the United Airlines crisis of April 2017 a masterclass in how not to apologise.

When United customer Dr David Dao was violently manhandled off his flight to make room for airline employees, videos filmed by shocked passengers spread rapidly across social media, sparking the mother of all PR headaches for United.

In response, the airline made a series of catastrophically clumsy moves, each compounding the original incident.

The initial 'apology' from CEO Oscar Munoz – in which he apologised only for having to 're-accommodate' customers, not for Dr Dao's injuries, was variously described as robotic, tone-deaf and insensitive. This was followed by a leaked internal message to United's staff which described the injured passenger as 'disruptive and belligerent' and praised them for following procedure (Business Insider, 2018).

In his second attempt, Munoz called the incident 'truly horrific' and offered his 'deepest apologies'. But it was too little, too late for United's reputation and its bottom line; the stock price had plummeted by $1 billion and 40 per cent of millennials said they would avoid travelling with United.

The lesson here for practitioners at all levels is *get it right first time* when customer service has fallen short. Apologise fast, apologise fully and apologise directly to those affected. Make sure you are apologising to the right audience; there's a line between defending your staff and adding insult to (in this case literal) injury.

As the United example shows, language and tone of voice are everything. Munoz's statements came across as contemptuous, insincere and uncaring.

Apologies must demonstrate empathy and they must be (or at least sound) genuine. It's worth remembering that (despite the march of AI into comms) 'Sorry, we got it wrong' is still an expression of remorse from one human being to another.

Maja Pawinska Sims is Associate Editor (EMEA) at The Holmes Report.

6.2. KEEPING THIRD PARTIES IN THE LOOP

Reporters are trained to seek comment and opinions from third parties. My editor called it 'a punch-up on the page'. The *BBC* calls it 'balance'. Either way, we can expect journalists to flesh out their story about our crisis by asking what experts and talking-heads think about it.

This is a good reason for keeping all our stakeholders informed, hour by hour. As a rule of thumb, tell them whatever you tell the media. It is much harder for people to be critical if a company has taken the trouble to keep them in the picture.

6.3. MEASURE OF SUCCESS

We can expect the media to be hard-nosed, aggressive and critical in a crisis. We should expect them to report what happened, what we are doing about it and what we say. accurately.

Our objective is fair and truthful coverage.

This will *probably* happen if we are seen to step forward, speak out and take control of events.

It will certainly not happen if the media believe we are hiding from them or trying to obstruct their quest for the facts. It will not happen if we say nothing, delay or issue meaningless statements.

As PR professionals, you know that media attention in a crisis is inevitable. *You* know that the media cannot be fobbed off and they won't go away.

Our challenge, very often, is to convince our clients and employers that being up-front and transparent is the *only* way to avert a 'PR disaster'.

Why the Media Don't Admire Corporate Crisis Behaviour

Jeremy Warner explained the media point of view in *The Telegraph*:

> @When confronting a crisis executives are too reluctant to accept wrong-doing and too slow to respond [...] especially in large companies unused to failure of any kind.'

Chris Blackhurst, writing in *The Independent*, said: 'A recurring mystery is the collective failure of the banks, with their armies of spin-doctors and reputation advisors, to see how others regard them and do something about it'.

The media drive crises. It's what they are meant to do.

Simon Caulkin in the *FT* pleaded with managers to use everyday English. 'Why is the language of management so

contorted? Why does so much of it seem to be about concealing meaning?'

He asked why plain speech in business is unusual. 'Companies that understand the force of straight talking are so rare that we are astonished when we find them' (*Financial Times*, 2011).

Kamal Ahmed, BBC Business Editor, said: 'VW is failing because the company doesn't speak human' (*PR Week*, 2015).

In a crisis, journalists make rapid judgements based largely on what the CEO says and does. If he or she is using 'management-speak' the media immediately assume they are obscuring the truth.

Journalists know that jargon, semi-legal phraseology and stilted constructions are a refuge.

Transparency and candour are solid gold if you want to get fair treatment from the media in a crisis. It starts with using normal, human language.

PR Oscars and Raspberries

For 20 years I've pressed my nose to the grindstone of news at Sky TV. As a Westminster correspondent I marvelled at Alastair Campbell's brass neck and alpha charisma. As a war reporter and now as a studio presenter I see the best and worst of crisis management. It's deeply subjective, of course, but Michael O'Leary's energetic effrontery wins my PR Oscar; Philip Green gets the raspberry.

I'm chary of throwing stones because I too have been in the eye of a media de-bagging. I know what it's like to feel the first stirrings of a Twitter-storm, watching aghast as the flames were fanned by the *Daily Mail*. Would the Prime Minister call for my resignation? It was David Cameron and he didn't demur, but then I saw how the social media mob can be re-directed.

For me the key was an exculpatory piece for the Media Guardian, written from my hotel room in Ukraine. I explained why I had picked up an item of luggage from an airliner shot down by the Russians. I described my emotional turmoil and apologised: I had crossed a line, I realised it at once and had said so, on-air.

It worked. On this occasion my crisis communications advisor was Mrs Brazier.

Colin Brazier presents news for Sky TV.

Summary

How the Media Drive Crises

A crisis is the media's best story. Competition is intense.

Verification can be sidelined in the heat of a crisis.

'We name the guilty men'.

Management often loses heart. 'How can we ever win?'.

Step forward, speak out and control the media agenda.

Avoid corporate-speak. Plain language wins sympathy.

The media expect CEOs to duck. Bravery gains respect.

CHAPTER 7

WORKING WITH LAWYERS

It can be depressing. All too often our best efforts to take the initiative with the media and other stakeholders are defeated by lawyers' advice to senior management. 'Say nothing'. Lawyers who give this advice rarely possess any media expertise or experience.

For whatever reason, legal advice usually trumps communications advice.

We can understand the lawyers' point of view. They are paid to minimise their client's risk. Since *all* public statements carry an element of risk – misreporting, misinterpretation, being taken out of context, being deliberately or innocently misunderstood – it often seems to make sense for a lawyer – whose main concern is risk avoidance – to advise our CEO to keep silent.

Lawyers are not paid to protect reputational assets, whereas we are.

7.1. EXPLAINING THE COMMUNICATIONS CASE TO LAWYERS

If the legal advice is to say nothing, we need to argue our case with the chief legal advisor (who may be in-house or may be an outside consultant). Some lawyers get the point at once. Others don't.

If this fails, we have to make the communications case – probably not for the first time – to the CEO. He or she has a difficult decision to make: how to balance the obvious desirability of speaking out, so as to at least partially control the media agenda, against the 'safe option' recommended by legal experts with all the authority of the law behind them.

It is twice as difficult for us if the legal advice is delivered to corporate managers at a remote head office in Chicago or Munich.

7.2. SPECIALIST MEDIA LAWYERS

One solution is to bring in a specialist media lawyer at the planning and preparation stage. He or she can present the case for using legal or regulatory means for making our statements more effectively and controlling the manner in which the media handle the story.

A media lawyer knows how the media work and how they make editorial decisions, which in crisis coverage usually involve a risk assessment. He or she knows how our organisation can minimise its own risk while still stepping up, speaking out and doing its best to preserve its reputation in fraught circumstances.

Ideally, an organisation's legal advisors and communications team should work in close collaboration. This is less rare than it once was.

A Perspective from Both Sides

In PR terms, I am a hybrid of two species who are normally at each other's throats.

For over 25 years I have undertaken reputation management for clients as diverse as multinationals, NGOs, financial institutions, politicians, celebrities and Royals. I have also legalled out material as varied as *South Park*, TV documentaries, fiction and non-fiction books, feature films and newsprint – though I have never acted for a 'Fleet Street' title.

I have also both prosecuted and defended privacy and defamation claims, as well as acting on both sides in regulatory disputes, dealing with both OFCOM and the PCC/IPSO.

All this experience leaves me in no doubt that the best approach in a media crisis is to combine top PR skills with the advice of *a lawyer who understands how editorial decisions are made*. This means a specialist – someone who (like myself) has spent years advising the media.

A PR consultancy has the benefit of a long-standing relationship with the client, so will understand the key messages that need to be communicated, cultural factors and so on. The lawyer will understand the legal framework which the media must observe.

There is much that can be achieved when – so to speak – both 'stick' and 'carrot' are engaged in crisis communications.

Jonathan Coad is a specialist media lawyer at Keystone Law.

Summary

Working with Lawyers

Lawyers are not responsible for corporate reputation; we are.

Lawyers typically advise 'Say nothing', which is fatal for reputation.

The CEO must balance PR advice against legal advice.

Involve a specialist media lawyer at the preparation stage.

Media lawyers understand the value of reputation.

Media lawyers know how the media evaluate their own risk.

Some media commentary can be legally curtailed.

CHAPTER 8

TACTICS AND TECHNIQUES

8.1. DECLARING A CRISIS

There is a moment in time when we have to decide: 'This is (or could be) a crisis. Put the crisis communications machinery in motion'. It's very disruptive: people have to stop doing their normal work, go somewhere else and start performing their crisis communications roles.

What triggers our decision? Very rarely, we hear from colleagues that something bad has happened. But not usually: negative news travels slowly in most organisations. As we saw in the Oxfam case, it is sometimes intentionally suppressed.

Most likely we will be alerted to a possible crisis by outside intervention. A tweet or post appears. We get a call from a journalist. Or both at the same time. It may happen at 3 am or on Boxing Day. There is no real down-time for a crisis communications team.

A crisis should be declared *by the CEO* (or accessible deputy) *on our advice*.

We have two communications priorities: to respond and to send a signal to all colleagues (especially front-line employees) telling them that, from now on, crisis SOPs apply.

What this means is that *no one says anything to anyone outside the organisation*. All questions and enquiries must be routed to the crisis communications team.

The objective is *secure communications*. It never works perfectly, but the SOPs help.

8.2. ACTION PLAN: WHO DOES WHAT?

The communications team members all need to know where to go and what to do when they get there. This is one reason why rehearsals and simulations pay dividends when a crisis actually happens. We do not want team members staring at us like rabbits in the headlights, waiting for instructions. We do not want our phones and inboxes jammed with questions from colleagues.

If our organisation has multiple sites, the crisis will very probably happen elsewhere. This means we need local communications people – permanent or temporary – to hold the fort. They must be trained and rehearsed. Crispin Manners emphasises the importance of a local response to a local crisis; employees, neighbours and local KOFs react more positively if the initial statement comes from someone they know.

Everyone should have a deputy in case the crisis hits when they are away.

Everyone needs a designated replacement in case the crisis is protracted, including ourselves. We can all manage a 24-hour shift if necessary, but who takes over when we need time out?

8.3. OPERATIONS AND COMMUNICATIONS

The people handling the physical crisis – working with the emergency services and so on – must be a separate team from the people handling communications with media and stakeholders.

The crisis may occur at head office, but it probably won't – so we need to think about liaison between the site of the crisis and our crisis communications centre.

CEOs often want to be in charge of operations, but they can't be; only the CEO is acceptable as a media spokesperson, so another senior figure needs to take charge of the physical aspects.

8.4. TEAMS, LOCATIONS AND RESOURCES

Our crisis communications team will usually be our day-to-day communications team. But there won't be enough of us, so we'll need to pull in temporary help from other departments to deal with the volume: monitoring, responding to enquiries, looking after people affected and relatives.

These helpers need advance briefing and training. They also need somewhere to work; ideally, a space large enough to accommodate everyone handling crisis communications. Most organisations commandeer the boardroom.

The team will need a lot of phones. It makes sense to keep spare phones in a box, charged up. We will also need plenty of screens to monitor online and social media, likewise radio and TV news broadcasts in real time. If the crisis has a local focus, as most do, we will need supplies of local media hot-off-the-press. We will also need petty cash.

8.5. PREPARING THE TEAM

A crisis is, by definition, unusual. It is not fair to expect our communications team to function well without training and practice. The stresses and strains of a crisis are unlike anything they will encounter in their everyday work.

It is often worth bringing in outside specialists to train the team, run rehearsals or simulations and help with the preparation of materials. Outsiders can advise on what's *essential* as opposed to *nice to have*. When budgets are stretched, this is useful.

Who will deal with the media at remote sites until we and our spokesperson can get there? People should be chosen and trained to perform this interim role.

Practice using the crisis communications centre. See if there are enough phones and screens. Will our team be able to handle door-stepping on the way home? What if our crisis takes a wholly unexpected turn? What if a containable crisis suddenly spins out of control? What if a senior political figure turns up without warning to address the cameras at the crisis site? How will we handle surprise events which escalate the crisis?

8.6. THE 'RED BOOK'

It's good practice to encapsulate what we and our colleagues need to know in a crisis communications manual. For historical reasons, this is often known as a 'Red Book'. A suggested list of contents is included in the Appendix.

The first part of the 'Red Book' sets out procedures: who does what, where and with what. Contact information. This section should be terse, so people will read and remember it.

The second part contains templates, background information, Fast Facts, graphics and photography – anything we will want to give the media in a crisis. Centralising this material saves time in a crisis, when time is at a premium.

Fast Facts are time-savers when dozens or perhaps hundreds of journalists who know nothing about our organisation are rushing to draft their stories. We don't want our team answering basic questions on the phone or by email.

Photographs: company portraits are usually cheerful, which is the wrong look in a crisis. We should get a special set of serious head-shots taken as part of our crisis communications preparation.

Format: the 'Red Book' should be available on our systems and also on flash-drives *and* in physical form. In a crisis, our systems may go down or we may not have access to them, so the physical file may be all we have.

Updating: a time-consuming chore, but obviously vital.

8.7. DARK SITES

The one thing we don't have in a crisis is time.

A good way to relieve the pressure is to provide the media with continuously refreshed information on a 'dark site'. This is a location where they can access our latest statements and also all the background information they need to put their stories together – pictures, maps, charts, facts and figures, details about the organisation/locations/products/services ...

Some organisations set up 'dark sites' with a separate URL and issue passwords. Others prefer to prepare a section of their website front page which is normally invisible but can be lit up in the case of a crisis. For most media, the website is their first port of call.

These microsites are aimed primarily at the media but can be used equally well to keep other stakeholders in the loop. Many stakeholders will automatically use their normal social media information sources to keep up with events, so our 'dark site' is an addition to, not a substitute for, issuing statements via these outlets.

8.8. ON THE DAY: THE 'GOLDEN HOUR'

A crisis is declared. *Action Stations!*

Our absolute number one priority is making sure that the people affected and their families are being looked after – not just by the emergency services but also by us. Everything we say about the crisis will stress that *those affected come first.*

We send a signal to all colleagues, especially those in the front line: it tells them that, from now on, crisis SOPs apply. What this means is that no one talks to any outsider without routing the enquiry through the crisis communications centre.

We compose and issue our initial statement. This must come from the CEO (or, if he or she is temporarily unavailable, from a designated deputy). It should ideally be delivered in person, at the site of the crisis, where cameras, mics and reporters will be gathering.

It should be issued simultaneously to all our other media contacts and stakeholders – in particular our own employees, who are often forgotten. It should appear at the same time on our 'dark site'.

If our CEO is elsewhere, we should arrange for him or her to get to the crisis site as soon as possible. We should accompany the CEO ourselves; from now on, our personal role is to help the CEO to decide what to do and say next.

We suspend normal brand and promotional campaigns.

The CEO announces our media update schedule. This is important. We want the media to realise from the word go that we intend to be open, transparent and helpful. They will draw the conclusion that we are behaving responsibly – not, as they often expect, trying to dodge and fudge. The CEO might say: 'Thank you. If there are no further questions …? I will be back here at (*names time an hour or two hours hence*) to provide our next update'.

It is likely that we won't have anything new for the CEO to say after one or two hours. It doesn't matter: the fact that he or she has set a schedule and is sticking to it tells the media that we are keeping our promise. Once they know that we mean what we say, there will be less pressure on our communications team.

The way our team behaves has a powerful effect on the way the media report the crisis. They don't yet know the facts and most of them don't know anything about our organisation. But they can tell in five seconds if we are doing our best to be professional and informative – in other words, trying to help them do their work. This behaviour can be hard to maintain under extreme pressure, but it pays: the media are much more likely to report the story even-handedly.

The 'Golden Hour'. It is sometimes said that we no longer have an hour – we must react in minutes. This is unwise: we need an hour to ascertain (as best we can) what is actually happening and to compose our initial statement using the right words and the right tone of voice. This is not easy at the best of times, still less when the phones are going mad and people are on the verge of panic. Our initial statement is incredibly important. It sets the scene for everything we will say and do throughout the crisis. We have an hour and we should use it.

The Last Word

The pressure of working through a crisis is intense. One of our challenges is maintaining a sense of perspective and context during the event – and *afterwards*.

It is hard to believe that no one else has been caught up in the crisis which you have been helping to manage. How could they not have seen what was going on – the drama, the tragedy , the scandal? More importantly, doesn't your experience give you valuable insights? The 'inside track' is a privileged position. You have learnt a lot which will be useful to others.

Could this be the final rule of good crisis management? When it is over, analyse what happened and learn from it; use your experience to help others.

For obvious reasons, don't talk about precise events, but draw lessons and general principles from what you saw working and not working.

Crisis case studies reveal the calculated nature of many decisions taken at the time to try to manage what was probably a media frenzy.

Even the best crisis communications management does not want to be remembered for its success. But it will be: search for 'Tylenol' and 'Tylenol Murders' is a top five result. Search 'British Midland' and the Kegworth Crash pops up immediately. Both these appalling tragedies are cited as textbook examples of good crisis management, but thirty years later both names are known for their disasters as much as for anything else.

Handle the crisis with the best possible professional skill and commitment. Learn from it and help others do the same.

Jackie Elliot is a former PRCA Chairman and Marketing Director of Rolex. She is now Senior Partner at Cathcart Consulting.

8.9. MAKING STATEMENTS

Those affected must come first.

Our spokesperson's initial statement should be rapid (an hour) and dynamic. It must make it obvious that he or she has strong personal feelings about what has happened *and* that he or she is firmly in charge of events, taking initiatives, determined to do everything possible to look after people whose health or welfare has been compromised and set on putting things right.

There are several 'formulae' for initial crisis statements. This is mine:

> *Recognise* that something has happened – or may have happened. We often don't know the facts in the 'Golden Hour'. The point is that our spokesperson is neither ducking nor denying: they are facing up to events and acting responsibly with the information at hand.
>
> *Regret* the consequences for those affected. Anyone whose life, health or welfare may have been impaired, and their families. This is all people really care about in a crisis, so it's the heart of our message. It is often said that the word 'sorry' can be taken as an admission of legal liability, but there is a world of difference between 'we are sorry for…' and 'we are sorry that…'.
>
> *Resolve* to (a) co-operate with the emergency services and authorities to sort the problem out as fast as possible

and/or (b) to conduct an internal investigation to find out what went wrong and make sure it can't happen again. Beware of letting the spokesperson claim responsibility for investigations which are actually the province of public authorities.

In most crises, *recognise-regret-resolve* is all that our spokesperson is able to say in their initial statement. But it's also all the world expects them to say.

Emotional Honesty Is the Key

Amid all the professional preparation, exercises and planning you need to do, it is sometimes easy to overlook what audiences respond to most when a crisis actually happens – namely its emotional impact.

Crises are usually tragedies, one way or another. Be sure to recognise this by saying what you have to say with genuine feeling. If not, all your best efforts are likely to be undermined.

People accept that errors and accidents happen from time to time. They are normally prepared to forgive them. What they are never prepared to forgive is a lack of emotion.

Your best crisis spokesperson will therefore not be the colleague who can read out prepared statements with complete calm and composure in the face of adversity. Your best spokesperson will be someone who can respond to what is in front of them with honesty and integrity – and also show their feelings.

In a real crisis people remember the emotional content more than finely crafted statements, no matter how smoothly they are delivered. It is better to pause and stumble – if you are showing what you genuinely feel – rather than to appear emotionless and cold.

Luke Blair is Director of Communications at Imperial College.

8.10. RAPID REBUTTAL

If a wrongly damaging or unfair comment appears in crisis reporting, we don't have time to observe the usual courtesies. If it stays up, uncorrected or undeleted, it will be copied by other media and will be part of the record for ever.

Call the editor and politely insist on a retraction. If that doesn't work, call a media lawyer.

8.11. FOLLOW-UP: FORGET NO ONE

Most of us can't wait to see the back of a crisis and get on with normal life. But there's an important final step once the heat dies down.

That gate-keeper at our logistics park who called us when a stranger bought him a pint at the White Lion and started asking questions... the third-party expert quoted in *The Times* saying that she knew our health-and-safety practices were state-of-the-art ... the reporter who spent hours interviewing everyone connected with the crisis and turned in a fair, balanced and well-informed piece ...

A note of appreciation is in order. If you don't feel happy thanking third parties for 'just doing their job' then – at least – acknowledge the contribution of colleagues like the gate-keeper. They have gone beyond the call of duty. We would like them to do the same thing next time we have a crisis.

8.12. LOG AND LEARN

All crises are different, so the steps we take to manage communications are partly experimental. One of our objectives is to hone and improve our systems, procedures and materials. A good way to tackle this is to keep a detailed record of what was done, what was said, how we responded to media commentary, how well it worked ...

This log gives us the opportunity to examine the sequence of events and make changes.

Easy to say; challenging when time and hands are in short supply. But worth it.

8.13. HANDLING TV INTERVIEWS IN A CRISIS

TV interviews can be nerve-wracking at the best of times. We are amateurs, the interviewer and the production team are professionals. We are conscious of being 'on-stage' in front of an audience who are not naturally sympathetic to company spokespeople. Many of us, thrust into this situation, end up looking stiff and uncomfortable; our words can come across as wooden or insincere.

In a crisis, the pressure on spokespeople is many times worse. Interviewers are inclined to suspect guilt and an effort to cover up, so they often feel entitled to go for the jugular.

Here are some recommendations:

Remember that 80 per cent of the impact a speaker makes is nothing to do with what they say or how they say it, but instead how they look and behave. Posture, gestures and body language are remembered when words are forgotten.

Costume matters. Men should wear a dark suit and a tie (even if they would never wear this kind of clothing on a normal working day). In a crisis, we need to show that we appreciate the gravity of the situation. For men and women, hair should be neat and off the face. Formality is the keynote.

Posture: upright, alert and attentive. Whether sitting or standing, keep hands together – no gestures. Lean very slightly forward to indicate helpfulness. Relax upper body. Our body language should demonstrate that we are serious and concerned (as we obviously are) and also that we are not frightened of facing the music.

Our voice should be in a lower register. We are talking about a tragedy, so a 'bright' tone sounds wrong. But avoid speaking in a monotone, because this can sound robotic. Observe the usual rules for interviews (half normal conversational speed and three-beat pauses between sentences). Give yourself time to reflect after each question – quick-fire replies sound mechanical – and keep eye-contact with the interviewer.

Language: ordinary, everyday words. Avoid at all costs 'corporate-speak' or legalese. Speak from the heart: all the audience cares about is the plight of the people who have been affected. They expect you to be emotionally involved, upstanding and determined to do whatever you can to help rectify the situation. Concerned and caring. Empathy.

Choosing the right words is the hardest part of a crisis media interview. Some spokespeople find it helpful to imagine they are not actually being interviewed but are, instead, being quizzed by a friend in the pub.

Hacks versus Flacks

All good jokes contain an element of truth, so the old PR gag about 'How many flacks does it take to change a light-bulb?' (answer: 'I don't know – can I get back to you on that?') is one of the funniest.

During my 25 years as a journalist, one of the most frustrating and infuriating experiences when dealing with the PR world is what could be called the good times/bad times dichotomy; when things are running smoothly, you are bombarded. When things turn sour, no one answers the phone.

I know the PR industry understands this issue and talks a lot about how to solve it. But it's shocking how often it still happens.

My advice to PR people is this: even if you have no response when things go pear-shaped, don't avoid the journalist. Instead, start some kind of dialogue. You could even say (if you must) that you'll get back to them. Much, much better than silence.

A very modern complaint is the tendency by new PR professionals to rely on email for communication with journalists. This has a mirror-image in journalism – young reporters are often guilty of relying too much on the internet and emailing sources with questions rather than calling them.

But it's impossible to pursue a story properly and investigate other lines of enquiry without getting on the phone and – ideally – meeting people face-to-face. In the same way, how can a PR person craft a pitch properly or manage a crisis effectively without having established a professional relationship with the journalist?

> In a crisis, media relationships are gold dust.
>
> *Nick Watson is a former* FT *correspondent and the founder of* Business New Europe.

Interaction with the interviewer: our sole function is to help the audience understand what has happened and what we are doing about it. We are there to provide information. For this reason, we should be attentive to the questions and make it obvious that we are doing our best to answer them, regardless of any antagonism or provocation on the part of the interviewer.

8.14. EXPRESSING REGRET

There are only so many ways the language allows us to say how much we regret what has happened to people in a crisis. We don't want to employ clichés or be thought to use time-worn formulations, because they can sound insincere. But ... neither should we be afraid of using words which have been used before: an effort to be original can make our words seem contrived.

The whole point of the initial statement is to create empathy. This means that the speaker (usually the CEO) is personally devastated by what has happened and is not afraid to express his or her feelings. This can be difficult for CEOs when this is not their normal style of speaking.

Here are some suggestions:

'We' is always better than 'I'. If need be, say: 'My colleagues and I at XYZ ...'. But it's much better to say: 'All of us here at XYZ ...' or 'Everyone at XYZ ...'

Never say: 'On behalf of ...' or 'The board of XYZ ...' This distances the speaker from what he or she is saying, which is the exact opposite of what we are trying to achieve.

Never say 'incident'. If people have been hurt (which is what defines a crisis) it's a tragedy, a disaster, an awful event, a calamity, an emergency, a dreadful shock ... we (the speaker) must try to see what has happened through the eyes of the people affected and their families... for them, it's traumatic to say the least.

Our words must express our fellow feeling. If we can get this right – and our words are only a small fraction of the impression that we (the speaker) will create – we have a chance of retaining their goodwill. If we sound hollow or insincere, they will mistrust and dislike us.

Some speakers can successfully use everyday language. 'Everyone here at XYZ is shattered about this ...' But only if it is their natural form of expression. It may not be; most CEOs are highly educated and not, almost by definition, ordinary folk.

'Our thoughts are with...' this is almost a cliché but it still works.

'We offer our condolences ...' best avoided. This isn't something people say in normal conversation. It sounds legal, corporate and unreal.

It is probably better to talk about what we are doing to help. Action versus mere phrases. '*We are all shocked by what has happened. I can't really put it into words. But I can tell you that dozens of people from XYZ have been coming into the office to see what they can do to help ... they are going out to visit the families right now and offering transport, accommodation ... whatever's needed ... we're doing everything we can to help the people – our passengers/customers/ tenants ....'*

> *We know how the families are feeling. There are no words for it. We are doing everything in our power to put things right for them, as best we can. Our people are at the scene right now, seeing what the relatives need. We don't know what caused the* crash/collapse/disaster *but that's not the point right now – the point is to see what we can do to help out ...*

There is a tendency for CEOs to use formal language when they are under stress or in the spotlight. When reported in a crisis, this makes them seem unfeeling and wooden. We should try to imagine what they would say to a friend – in a bar or a pub – when talking about how they felt. It is feelings rather than facts which make people like and trust CEOs in a crisis.

> *There's only one thing that matters for XYZ right now: doing whatever we can to look after the families of the people in the* crash/collapse/fire. *We've got people on the spot as I speak. They have money and authority to sort things out for the wives and children and they'll be there for as long as it takes ....*

We assume that the CEO needs to make a 'formal statement'. Is this true? Isn't it better for the CEO to speak from the heart? Lawyers will usually argue for a rather cold, corporate initial statement. Their thoughts are focussed on liability. *Our* thoughts are devoted to corporate reputation, which means that people like us. Formality will not achieve this.

> *There can't be anything worse than having your husband/brother killed/injured in an accident like this. It's heartbreaking. No-one at XYZ is doing anything right now except trying to make things a bit better for all the relatives and friends ...*
>
> *When something like this happens we forget everything else. The only thing that matters is doing whatever we can for the families of the people who have been hurt/injured. All I can tell you is that everyone at XYZ has dropped whatever they were doing and is seeing what they can do to help the people affected by this* accident/disaster/crash ...
>
> *There's only one thought in our minds at XYZ right now... what can we do to help the families and friends of the people who were injured? We've got people on the spot whose only priority is to see how we can help ... Do they need accommodation? Do they need money? Do they need food? What do they need?* Whatever *they need we have people who can provide it ...*

All this assumes that the CEO actually feels a sense of personal responsibility for what has happened. Hopefully this is true. It is almost impossible to fake sincerity in front of a camera.

The Human Element

Aside from the obvious planning scenarios, preparation, background information and all the other things that communications teams can think about in advance, there is always the detail of the moment. That's when agile teams need to think on their feet, be sensitive to external factors and ensure they act accordingly.

Consider the news agenda of the day and whether or not it has any bearing on how you present your response.

If a spokesperson is appropriate, be selective from those you have prepared for such a scenario. Pay attention to details like style and clothing – these factors are memorable.

But, most importantly, in everything you do – *think human*. How will this sound? How will this be perceived? How will this play out across kitchen tables around the country?

Of course, your response must be the facts – the truth – the now. But beyond that corporations, for all their scenario planning, too often present with great *authority* when *empathy* is the word of the moment. They too often get bogged down in technical language and jargon which can be confusing and at worst, sound evasive.

Alison Clarke is the Principal of Alison Clarke Communications.

Cool, Calm and Collected

In a crisis, the instinct of many people is to panic. They either want to rush to say something without thinking or they want to hide away and say nothing. Some will want to hit out at critics. Others will seek to pass on responsibility to others. While these reactions are understandable, they are not advisable.

In today's world of social media, it can be hard to remember that the majority of the general public are reasonable people. They are not zealots or passionate single-issue campaigners. They recognise that the world is not black and white. If you demonstrate that you, too, are reasonable you have a chance of overcoming the situation and maintaining a positive public perception.

Your response should use language that people can relate to. Avoid jargon, management-speak or technical terminology.

Speculation is the life-blood of the media so stick to what you know. Don't be tempted to fill a vacuum by making statements that could come back to bite you later.

To be reasonable you have to recognise what has gone wrong, empathise with those affected and take responsibility for what you can control.

Be clear about what you will be doing to resolve the situation and be concise, so that there can be absolutely no doubt about what you are saying.

Leigh Bramall is a Director at Counter Context.

Summary

Making Statements

The affected must come first in our actions and statements.

Initial statement: recognise, regret resolve.

Rapid rebuttal for incorrect or unfair media coverage.

Set our own timetable for updates and stick to it.

Inform stakeholders and third parties: keep them informed.

Tone of voice: calm, concerned, human and in control; empathy.

Language: plain, straightforward and warm.

Summary

Tactics and Techniques

Decide in advance who declares a crisis and how.

Plan who does what, where and with what resources.

Keep crisis operations separate from crisis communications.

Train the communications team: monitoring, drafting and responding.

Compile a 'Red Book' and keep it up to date.

Set up a 'dark site'.

On the day, seize the 'Golden Hour' and keep the initiative.

CHAPTER 9

SPOKESPEOPLE

The performance of our spokesperson is critical. If they do well, we will probably come out of the crisis unscathed. If they do poorly, we are very likely to suffer reputational damage.

Is it really as simple as that? Nine times out of 10, yes.

The media pride themselves on *getting the facts*. We admire them for this, but in reality most media coverage in a crisis is impressionistic. No one really *knows* the facts, which might only emerge months or years later.

The key factor in media coverage of a crisis – positive, neutral, negative or hostile – is what they *feel* about the spokesperson's sincerity, humanity and competence under pressure.

9.1. IT *HAS* TO BE THE CEO

It used to be acceptable for an anonymous 'spokesperson' to issue statements and be quoted in the media, verbatim. This still happens, occasionally, but today's media are less inclined to tolerate anyone other than the top man or woman speaking on behalf of an organisation in a crisis.

It's obvious why. Readers, viewers, listeners and browsers want to know what *Richard Branson* said when his spaceship crashed. They want to hear how *Philip Green* explained the collapse of BHS. They want to see what *Michael Dell* has to say about his laptops going up in smoke. They would like to hear how *Willie Walsh* apologises for their lost luggage.

It doesn't matter if Willie Walsh has no personal responsibility for British Airway's luggage systems. We live in a world where most news is simplified. It's a world of brands and the CEO – like it or not – is part of the corporate brand; in a crisis, he or she is the *only* part that really matters to the media.

9.2. HOW WE CAN SUPPORT OUR CEO

We may have a day-to-day business relationship with the CEO, but we may not: we quite likely report to another board member with responsibility for marketing or corporate affairs. In a crisis, *we* must be at the CEO's right hand. Our personal role is to help the CEO decide what to do and say next, and make sure he or she has all the advice they need to perform well.

This starts early in the planning process. The CEO must 'buy-in' to the need to front crisis communications in person. Persuading the CEO often presents difficulties – it's not a duty that many CEOs welcome. There are arguments throughout this book which will, we hope, help you make the case successfully.

Once on-board, the CEO should be invited to participate in contingency brainstorms. This makes the possibility of a crisis and their own role in it more real. We should involve the CEO in other crisis preparation decisions discussed elsewhere in this book – for instance, who their deputy should be and how crisis SOPs should be declared.

9.3. CRISIS MEDIA TRAINING

The CEO (and other spokespeople we may call on in a crisis) needs *crisis-specific* media training. This is unlike 'normal' media training, which they have – hopefully – already received.

Our objective with ordinary media training is to get our spokespeople to sit up properly, keep a pleasant expression on their faces, avoid waffle, speak in everyday language and – ideally – mention the brand at least once. Our aim is to instil some basic techniques and enhance their confidence.

In a crisis, the media can behave completely differently; they can be hostile, aggressive, provocative, challenging and even rude. Their role model is John Humphrys.

It is unfair to expose our spokespeople to this kind of harrowing interview without practice. For this reason, they should receive *crisis-specific* media training, based on our 'Worst of the Worst' contingencies, with a three-hour refresher session at least once a year.

9.4. REHEARSALS AND SIMULATIONS

Our communications team need crisis rehearsals and these should involve our designated spokespeople. Large companies who take crisis preparation seriously invest substantial amounts of time, effort and money in staging simulations – partly to see how their systems and processes can be improved, partly to give their front-line communicators an insight into the pressure, disruption and mayhem which usually ensues.

Rehearsals can be put in everyone's calendar but simulations should be a surprise.

Most large agencies can organise crisis simulations and there are also specialist firms – like Polpeo, a PRCA partner – who can be brought in to handle the entire project from A to Z. I have never met a company who didn't think that crisis rehearsals and simulations were not money well spent.

9.5. SPOKESPEOPLE'S LANGUAGE

We have all heard it: a CEO in the hot seat who looks at the camera with a fixed grimace and speaks in a strange, wooden fashion – a bit like a robot. Their language is stiff and contorted, a weird mixture of legalese and corporate-speak. They have our sympathy; they are trying to do something difficult and stressful without practice, probably without training, and they freeze; they are unable to talk like a normal human being – the *very thing* which is essential in a crisis.

When this happens the organisation's communications professionals have failed.

It is our job to train, coach and rehearse our spokespeople until they can come across in an interview as a person the audience will like, respect and believe in. A lot of this depends on body language and behaviour. A lot depends on everyday language – free of jargon, devoid of technical obscurity, the kind of vocabulary and construction our spokespeople use when chatting to their friends.

This is not easy when spokespeople feel that their heads are on the block. I make no apology for repeating this recommendation: time spent on spokesperson training, rehearsal and simulation is money in the bank when a crisis strikes.

The Political Dimension

It is difficult to imagine any kind of a crisis that does not have a political dimension. On that basis, it is equally almost impossible to imagine a crisis that does not require at least some degree of public affairs input. Public affairs involvement – either from in-house resource or through consultancy – is essential in any crisis comms situation.

Whatever the nature of your crisis, politicians can help you or hammer you – possibly even both. Public affairs is all about threat – and opportunity. Crisis comms relates more to the former than the latter, but some crises can be turned around and converted in to an opportunity.

So whether you are dealing with industrial action, a factory closure, a redundancy programme, a health and safety issue, a natural disaster, an anticipated or an unanticipated crisis, there will be politicians who either have no choice but to engage, or who choose to do so. How they intervene can be influenced and shaped, most easily by public affairs professionals they know and trust. By deploying standard public affairs techniques misconceptions can be rectified, vehement critics can be mollified and supporters can be identified, briefed and deployed as spokespersons or advocates.

The effects of some crises can be ameliorated, in a damage limitation exercise. Others can be effectively managed and some can even be turned around. On occasion, it is even possible that a crisis can be used as a catalyst to introduce much-needed changes or reforms. After all, as Winston

Churchill, one of the greatest politicians (and greatest crisis managers) in history once said – 'Never let a good crisis go to waste'.

Lionel Zetter is a Public Affairs Consultant, Author and Trainer. He is a member of the PRCA Training faculty. He is also the owner of Shepherd's in Marsham Street, a favourite restaurant among politicians.

Crisis Communications in the City

Avoid turning a drama into a crisis. Knee-jerking into releasing a statement may cause unnecessary damage. The issue may not have achieved real traction, so holding a reactive statement at the ready may be all that's required. Any quote is noise, so avoid if at all possible.

If the drama has the potential to become a full-blown crisis, issuing a statement too early doesn't help; it attracts attention and raises more questions than can be answered. It's a fine judgement. Getting ahead of a situation is always desirable but fanning the flames is not.

If the situation has market abuse connotations, 'materiality' over-rides caution. The Financial Conduct Authority will investigate who knew what in the context of the timing of a statement. But where the material outcome (causing share-price movement) is not yet quantifiable, issuing an inconclusive statement could be judged as in itself, potentially misleading the market. Another fine call.

Whether preparing for or dealing with a live situation, getting to the truth is critical. A management unwilling to countenance awkward, unpleasant questions will ultimately be found out and punished accordingly. Go on asking the questions until you (1) understand the answers and (2) believe them.

Do not back off until then. *Your* reputation is on the line. If the crisis is raging, remember that people always come first – health, livelihoods. The CEO must attend the site – if there is one – and be ready to face the cameras/mics. A credible apology, spoken genuinely – not read out – goes a long way.

Managing a crisis successfully is about *control*. Preferably a single spokesperson. A very small group at the centre making the judgements and only involving other people when necessary. That small group should have an up-to-date file at hand which identifies key stakeholders, contacts and so on. And you'll need someone who knows how to manage conference calls ....

Alex Sandberg founded College Hill (now Instinctif) and continues to consult through his company Averdant.

Summary

Spokespeople

The spokesperson's performance is critical.

It has to be the CEO. He or she must get to the site immediately.

The spokesperson needs our full-time support.

Crisis-specific media training is vital (not normal media training).

Rehearsals and simulations help CEOs react well under unusual stress.

CEOs must be shown how a good crisis performance enhances reputation.

Examples: Lord Browne, Sir Richard Branson and Dara Khosrowshahi.

CHAPTER 10

ONLINE AND SOCIAL

This is a moving target. We admired the way Barack Obama's team used social media in his election campaign, but who guessed in 2008 that his successor would use Twitter to communicate directly with (apparently) 50 million followers?

We liked the Page and Brin mantra: 'Don't be evil'. Now we're not so sure. We thought Facebook was a Good Thing until March 2018. Now we are wondering.

Here are some crisis communications management principles which – at the time of writing – may be helpful in managing a problem which emerges via online or social media.

10.1. WHAT'S DIFFERENT?

The usual answers are *speed* and *scale*.

Is this right? The real damage to a corporate or brand reputation comes when a problem that starts on social media gravitates to TV, radio and branded media outlets. Which may happen, or may not.

Most people know that social media is the natural habitat of fake news and nonsense. But it's also the source of real issues which can and do migrate to serious news outlets.

When a negative item appears on social media we have to decide if it's *real* and, if so, whether or not it is likely to proliferate. Will it stand up to scrutiny from branded media?

Is it a real problem – and possibly a crisis – or is it just more 'electronic confetti'? *The Verification Handbook* (Silverman, 2018), referenced in 'Further Resources', is used by the media themselves and is invaluable.

We have more time than we imagine. We have an hour – the 'Golden Hour' – at least.

It is a mistake to imagine that we have to respond in minutes. If we hurry, we run a real risk of getting it wrong. We should take time to compose our response (if any).

Scale? Managers are often impressed and sometimes frightened by numbers with six zeros. How many of these numbers matter – even if they are real and we know that half of them are probably bots? There are only a handful of social news systems that *really* count. How many online news outlets carry true authority? As a rule of thumb, if they behave like conventional branded media (*we know who writes them, we can talk to them*) we should take them seriously. If not, not.

10.2. FIRST VERIFY, THEN – MAYBE – RESPOND

Is it real? If so, is it a customer complaint? Most organisations have methods in place to handle complaints sensitively and effectively. This is not a crisis (yet).

Is it fake? Is it a Photoshop picture conjured up by a competitor, or, more likely, by someone with a warped sense of humour? There are measures we should take – but they do not involve crisis communications management.

Is it an example of angry, over-wrought online unpleasantness posted by people with too much time on their hands? The internet is full of this stuff. We should take a realistic view. Management tend to be over-sensitive to online and social criticism. Our role is to give them realistic advice.

Or … in our opinion, is this a genuine issue which is likely to be picked up by branded media outlets and do us reputational harm? It's a judgement call. Making the *right* decision needs experience.

10.3. POINTS TO CONSIDER IN ADVANCE

Server capacity: it may not be adequate to deal with an online onslaught, especially if a flood or fire has put systems out of action. We may need back-up. What happens if there is a power outage?

We can register likely flame URLs and hashtags ourselves, denying them to online opponents.

Link channels: install a system which can deliver updates to all our owned channels – website, Facebook page, intranet/Wiki, company blogs and so on – from a single input.

Ensure monitoring and alert systems are efficient. There are free services and others available on subscription. We get what we pay for. Volunteer monitors among our own colleagues can be extremely effective (and we will need a 24-hour hotline – which means *us*).

10.4. RESPONDING ONLINE

There is not much time (an hour). The first responder's role is crucial. Composing our first response should be the responsibility of an experienced and senior communications professional.

Tone: all-important. Calm, concerned, active and human.

Use attack title or hashtag to ensure co-location of response.

We can amplify our response (which an attacker can't) using owned media, other online media and the mainstream media (MSM). Do we have influencers on-board? They can help.

Quell speculation. Piquant lies spread quickly. We all know how Tiger Woods checked himself into a sex clinic for therapy. He never did. It was a complete fabrication, but people liked the story and shared it. Our best defence is to issue a measured reply, fast, whenever and wherever untrue speculation appears in our list of influential, authentic and branded news outlets.

Our own website and Facebook page are super-important. That's where the media will look first.

We should keep employees informed using our intranet or wiki. We can also provide content for use by colleagues with their own sites, blogs and pages.

If it's looking like a crisis, cancel all online/social promotions. The media love to juxtapose brands in trouble with happy, up-beat marketing content which is inadvertently still running.

Never delete responses. Management often demand that everything connected to a crisis is taken down as soon as it all seems to be over. This is a bad mistake: it means that the attack or criticism will stay up forever while our explanation has vanished.

Ten Steps for Managing a Digital Crisis

Undertake a *digital* audit of your brand's ability to deal with a *digital* crisis. What plans are in place? How robust are they? Has your team had digital comms training? What systems exist?

Build a brand tribe: the most successful brands in the social media world devote effort to building their own brand tribes. These are groups of people who are linked by a shared belief around a brand. They are not simply consumers – they are also believers in, and promoters of, the brand. A brand tribe is capable of collective action and can therefore be a powerful defence in the digital field when a brand comes under attack.

Know your antagonists: once you know who your antagonists are and understand their motivations you can quickly develop a response. Establish now who the digital influencers are in your field and where the hate-sites, spoof-sites and anti-sites are located.

Staff awareness: most crises we see in the digital world are typically internally triggered – poor customer service, poor marketing practices, poor public or influencer relations, poor governance. Staff awareness and training are vital: staff need to know that, in the digital world, the brand is always on stage.

Vigilance: invest in the appropriate online listening tools to monitor activity around your brand's reputation and profile. Understand which hashtags will be used in connection with your brand's activities.

Plan for response: whenever possible engage with antagonists but do so off-line in a private situation. However, it may sometimes be better – for instance, in a Twitter Storm – to let it blow over first; getting involved may make the situation worse. Be careful about how you call it.

Location, location, location: when a crisis unfolds location becomes vital. Use the same hashtags and keywords to get close to your antagonist's content. If you can, swap links with them. Consider sponsored links.

Create a dark site: a dark site should be the cornerstone of your strategy. It's a website or web-page which is only activated in a crisis but has FAQs or initial statements already established. A separate URL will allow your main website to deal with everyday business while the dark site handles the crisis.

Be proactive: publish as much positive content as possible in order to push down negative news in the search rankings. Use a corporate blog and YouTube channel to publish content consistently with special emphasis on keywords, imagery and video.

Have a strategy: to quote the old Roman saying: 'If you want peace prepare for war'. Prepare a crisis management team structure today. Keep reporting lines as short as possible. Prepare as many scenarios as possible and practise operating against each one.

Steve Dunne is the CEO of Digital Drums and a member of the PRCA Training faculty.

Summary

Online and Social

Monitoring: free, subscription and volunteer?

Triage: is it real? Use *Verification Handbook* to authenticate.

Only react to branded online outlets.

Don't rush. We have an hour and we need an hour.

Tone: response should be composed by a senior and experienced communicator.

Consider server capacity in advance. Own likely critical URLs and hashtags.

Use owned and MSM to amplify response.

CHAPTER 11

EVALUATION AND LEARNING

When a crisis fades away there is a tendency for most of us – and especially our managers and clients – to say: 'Thank goodness that's over! Now – back to normal business.'

Understandable, but we should take the time to assess what we did and how well it worked.

We can judge the overall success of our work by looking at numbers:

- How did the share price move? Typically, prices will dip as soon as a crisis hits the news media, but what we are looking for is a firming-up, sooner rather than later, which tells us that the markets feel we are on top of the episode and performing creditably.
- Did trade orders fluctuate? If so, how soon did normal levels resume?
- How did employee morale respond? Most HR departments have dashboards which tell us day by day, or week by week, if management are retaining employees' confidence.

- HR will also have records of the volume and quality of recruitment applications. If these maintain their expected levels, we have succeeded in protecting corporate reputation among this highly sensitive stakeholder group.
- KOFs and KDMs: have their sentiments towards our organisation taken a negative turn? We can tell by running randomised Familiarity/Favourability surveys during the life of the crisis. Many organisations keep track of KOF/KDM perceptions on a routine basis using Fam/Fav surveys and Net Promoter Score studies among customers and clients.

11.1. ASSESSING MEDIA COVERAGE

There are two criteria: (1) was the media coverage broadly accurate? In a crisis, the media are often tempted to speculate and occasionally, fabricate. If we have kept these two demons at bay we can be confident that our media outreach has been positive, proactive and acceptable.

(2) Was the media coverage broadly sympathetic – somewhere between neutral and positive? If so, it means that our performance, and that of our spokespeople, have convinced the media that we made a genuine effort to solve the crisis in the right way and that we also made an effort to help them do their job as journalists.

If not, it reflects the media's opinion of our competence and transparency.

11.2. EVALUATING OUR PERFORMANCE

Those are the outputs and results. What about the inputs?

How did the communications team perform? Working under extreme stress is probably a new experience for many of them. Did they hold up? What did we learn about the efficiency of our systems, technology and resources? What needs changing?

Did we get co-operation from other parts of the organisation? If not, how can we improve things so that we receive quicker, more useful help from colleagues in future? Do we need a CEO edict?

Were our media and stakeholder materials fit for purpose? Or did we find ourselves hurrying to produce background information in the heat of the crisis?

Was our monitoring system good enough? Did we know what the media and other commentators were saying, minute by minute? Did we feel we were able to keep on top of the media agenda?

11.3. EVALUATING SPOKESPEOPLE'S PERFORMANCE

We know that our spokespeople's performance is critical to our ability to survive a crisis. The media expect the CEO to be the face and voice of the organisation in adversity; they will make many of their judgements, if not all, based solely on the CEO's availability, credibility, empathy and evident ability to resolve the situation.

- Did the CEO put crisis communications front-and-centre?
- Did he/she demonstrate courage in facing the media when there was a strong temptation to duck?
- Did he/she speak naturally, like a human being or take refuge in quasi-legal or technical language?
- Did he/she really seem to care about the people affected and did this come across to the media?

- Does he or she have a realistic opinion of their own performance in hindsight?

It can (obviously) be difficult to criticise the performance of a CEO, especially when he or she has just been through a torrid experience. But we must give honest feedback, diplomatically. It may be the case (and it almost always is) that the CEO would benefit from another round of crisis-specific media training. If we are lucky, the CEO may be the first to suggest it.

11.4. WHY EVALUATE?

There is no routine in crisis communications. Every crisis is different and comes, by definition, as a surprise. We prepare as best we can but, inevitably, we will meet unforeseen problems.

This is the point of evaluation. What worked well? What didn't? What caught us unprepared? A thorough post-mortem will equip us to do better next time.

Because, unless our firm is a statistical anomaly, there *will* be a next time.

Summary

Evaluation and Learning

Monitor numbers: share price, trade orders, employee morale and KOF sentiment.

Media coverage: was it generally accurate and fair?

How was our communications team's performance? What did we learn?

How was our spokesperson's performance? How could it have been better?

How were our systems, processes and materials? Can they be improved?

What caught us by surprise?

It's worth a post-mortem. There will be another crisis, one day.

CHAPTER 12

WHAT WOULD WE HAVE DONE?

It can be useful to examine how organisations handle crisis communications in the glare of the media spotlight. The initial statement is almost always the key factor in determining whether or not the organisation emerges with credit.

Here are some examples. If we had been advising the CEO, what would we have said?

12.1. DEATH AT A ZOO

A female zoo-keeper was killed by a tiger at the Terra Natura Zoo in Benidorm. The zoo's management issued a statement the next day. It was carried by most of the world's media.

> *We offer our deep condolences to the family and friends of the keeper who will be deeply missed by staff at the zoo where she worked for eight years as a specialist in felines. We are all shocked by this tragedy. Terra Natura observes strict guidelines on security for the management of animals.*

> *For reasons which are being investigated the member of staff came directly into contact with the animals while she was cleaning out a cage area. (*Daily Mirror, *2016)*

Oddly, the keeper is not named. There may be a good reason for this. The statement is adequate, but could we have done better? What would we have said?

12.2. GIVING THE GAME AWAY

Hinkley Point receives massive amounts of media coverage, mostly critical. Jennifer Rankin in *The Guardian* scored a bull's-eye when she managed to get a member of the construction staff to condemn the reactor's design:

> *Unsurprisingly, nuclear workers take a close interest in the EPR's fortunes. Philippe Revel, a 51-year-old foreman, is not convinced that the much-vaunted next-generation model is an improvement on its simpler, more functional predecessors, or that it will play a big role in France's nuclear future. Asked whether he would recommend it to the British, he smiles wryly: 'Personally, no. It is too complicated. It is too big. (*The Guardian, *2016)*

This one is hard to ignore. If you worked in comms for DECC, EDF or Areva, how would you respond?

12.3. BA: ONE THING AFTER ANOTHER

British Airways is a commercial success story but its PR has been described as maladroit (*Weyer*, 2017).

> *BA had a narrow window to be candid. It is astonishing that management seemed not to understand this (*Evening Standard, *2017).*

> *BA's crisis communications seems to have added to customer frustrations rather than alleviating them (ContinuityCentral.com, 2017).*

> *Failure is one thing. The response is something else. (Denis Fischbacker-Smith, Glasgow University)*

> *BA is stuck in a branding no-man's land. (Peter Duncan, Message Matters)*

How would you encapsulate a new and more effective crisis communications strategy for BA?

12.4. SAMSUNG: CAUGHT OUT IN THE Q&A

Koh Dong-Jin (usually a very able corporate communicator) gave a press briefing after the Galaxy Note 7 'explosions' story went viral.

> *We are deeply sorry for causing concern and inconvenience among our users.*

In the Q&A he was asked what the recall would cost the company.

> *A big amount [...] that is heart-breaking. (*The Times, *2016)*

His words tell us, inadvertently, about Samsung's real corporate values.

What can Mr Koh say to recover from this gaffe?

12.5. CHEVRON'S APOLOGY: COKE AND PIZZA

A Chevron well exploded in Dunkard, Pennsylvania, killing one worker and causing a fire which blazed for five days.

Chevron's apology took the form of a letter to residents with a coupon for a free pizza and a bottle of soda.

Local people went online to protest. Chevron reacted by criticising local people and censoring negative posts on their social media. The story then went viral (Gawker.com, 2014).

What should Chevron have done after their well exploded? Why didn't they?

12.6. THOMAS COOK: 'NO NEED TO APOLOGISE'

In 2006, two children died in a Corfu villa from carbon monoxide poisoning.

In 2015, it emerged that Thomas Cook had received €3m in compensation from the property owner's insurance company. When this news hit the media Thomas Cook gave €1.5m to UNICEF. They claimed they had sent a letter of apology to the children's parents, who said the first they heard of it was when they were shown the letter by reporters.

> *Peter Fankhauser, CEO since 2014, said: '[...] but there's no need to apologise because there was no wrong-doing by Thomas Cook [...]'*

> *The media said: 'It might have been legally correct but it was a catastrophically callous tone to take'*

> *At every turn, Thomas Cook's engagement with the parents has been tardy, robotic and begrudging. (BBC.com, 2015)*

What should Mr Fankhauser have said and done when the story broke?

12.7. STARBUCKS' £25 MILLION GIFT TO HMRC

Starbucks came under fire in 2012 – along with Amazon, Google and Apple – for not paying the right amount of UK taxes. Starbucks' high-street presence ensured that they bore the brunt of demonstrations and boycotts.

Starbucks decided to make a donation of £25m to the UK Treasury (*The Guardian*, 2015).

No one knew what to make of this. Was £25m a lot, a little or the right amount?

Observers pointed out that the people responsible for minimising Starbucks' tax probably never met the people responsible for the brand's reputation.

How would you advise companies like Starbucks to avoid this kind of PR disaster?

12.8. MORRISONS' DATA-BREACH

Morrisons' new CEO, Dalton Philips, gave a media briefing about improved IT systems in March 2014. Hours later details of salaries, bank accounts and home addresses for thousands of Morrisons' staff were posted online and sent to the Bradford *Telegraph and Argus*.

Morrisons contacted staff by email and via their Facebook page to tell them about the problem. Staff went online to express their anger: *Good communications, Morrisons! Reading about this on Facebook does not inspire confidence* (*The Independent*, 2017). The story went viral and mainstream.

How should Morrisons have told their people? Why didn't they?

12.9. GM: 'A RISK YOU SOMETIMES TAKE'

GM had to recall 1.3 million cars when steering mechanism malfunctions were linked to 14 crashes.

Bob Lutz, a GM head of division, said: 'This is a risk you sometimes take when you buy a complete system from a supplier' (BBC.com, 2010).

Who is 'you'?

Why did he say this, and why is it always a bad idea to blame a supplier?

12.10. MA AILUN'S iPHONE CHARGER

Ma Ailun was electrocuted while using her iPhone that was connected to the socket with a charger cable (which turned out to be a counterfeit).

Her sister posted: 'We hope that Apple can give us an explanation. Also, that all of you will refrain from using your mobile devices while charging'.

Apple issued a statement via Reuters: *We are deeply saddened to learn of this tragic incident and offer our condolences to the Ma family. We will fully investigate and co-operate with the authorities in this matter* (*Daily Telegraph*, 2013).

Maybe not quite what we would expect from the world's favourite love-brand.

How would you have expressed Apple's initial statement?

12.11. VW'S DIESEL CHEAT DEVICE

This continuing saga has badly damaged the reputation of one of the world's most admired car companies.

As often happens, the way that VW handled its communications became the story.

Graham Ruddick in *The Guardian* criticised VW's missed opportunity to say something meaningful at the AGM in 2015: *A pledge to be transparent, while at the same time saying nothing (Fortune*, 2018).

Kamel Ahmed, BBCTV's Business Editor, was blunter: *VW is failing because the company doesn't speak human.*

VW is not alone. Why do large, successful companies so often find it hard to 'speak human'?

12.12. NICK VARNEY DOES WELL ... THEN NOT SO WELL

A nightmare unfolded at Alton Towers when the 'Smiler' crashed and injured five people in June 2015. Two young women had their legs amputated. Merlin was later fined £5m for health and safety breaches.

Nick Varney, Merlin's CEO, was initially judged to have done well, especially when he gave a spirited defence under attack from Kay Burley on *Sky News*.

In September he visited Vicky Balch, a 20-year-old who had lost a leg in the crash, and mentioned that the company 'was losing a lot of money'. Ms Balch was not impressed and told the media. Varney's apparent heartlessness then became the story (*Daily Mail*, 2015).

Could any amount of media training have protected Varney from making this mistake? If you had been advising Merlin in the aftermath, what would you recommend that he should say?

12.13. UNITED AIRLINES DRAGS A PASSENGER OFF THE PLANE

We all saw clips of a passenger, his face bloody, being hauled off a United Airlines flight when he refused to surrender his seat in April 2017. It turned out that United needed to move four of their own staff to another airport. Three passengers accepted their fate but Dr Dao didn't.

Oscar Munoz, United's CEO, initially tried to blame Dr Dao for being – as he put it – 'belligerent and disruptive'. But the world had seen the clips and knew this was not true.

Munoz used strange language, talking about the necessity to 're-accommodate customers'. It was two days before he managed to issue an apology (*PRWeek*, 2017).

Roomy Khan in Forbes drew attention to Munoz's probable priority; keeping United's staff happy. He had, after all, won US *PRWeek*'s Award as Communicator of the Year.

How could a seasoned CEO make such a catastrophic mistake?

12.14. OXFAM: TURNING A CRISIS INTO A CATASTROPHE

In February 2018, *The Times* revealed that Oxfam had covered up a whistleblower's report on sexual abuse by staff in the aftermath of the 2010 Haiti earthquake. The account was lurid ... 'girls wearing Oxfam T-shirts running around half-naked ...' It was also very serious, alleging rape, harassment and possible under-age sex. Oxfam let six staff and its country director, Roland van Hauwermeiren, leave quietly. Hauwermeiren went on to a similar job with Action Against Hunger in Bangladesh.

The crisis was picked up, pursued and enlarged by other media. Oxfam's deputy CEO resigned. Its Head of Safeguarding at the time of the Haiti scandal, Helen Evans, said she had *tried* to escalate the Haiti report to Oxfam's senior management. MPs and commentators of all stripes expressed disgust, shock and outrage.

Enter Mark Goldring, Oxfam's CEO. In possibly the worst crisis interviews on record, he told us that the last six days had been the most intense and challenging of his life. He had not been able to sleep. Then: 'We've been savaged [...] what did we do? We murdered babies in their cots?'

Facing the International Development Committee in the House of Commons he later apologised: 'I shouldn't have put my own sleep, or lack of it, in the public domain.' (*The Times*, 2018).

The Oxfam case raises many questions and severely damaged the 'licence to operate' of this venerable charity. For professional communicators one of the most puzzling questions is: how could a large and sophisticated organisation like Oxfam allow its CEO to speak to the media without guidance, support or – apparently – any kind of preparation?

AFTERWORD

Between the crisis and the catastrophe there is always time for a glass of champagne.

Paul Claudel, French Ambassador,
on the eve of the Wall Street Crash (1929)

Prevarication is not an option in a crisis.

General Hermann von Stein,
Defender of Thiepval (1916)

APPENDIX

A.1. A STAKEHOLDER CHECKLIST

(1) **Those affected**
- People directly affected and their families

(2) **Corporate stakeholders**
- staff and their families (NB unions and staff associations);
- local, regional, national and international management;
- specialist departments: legal, financial, HR and marketing;
- trade customers and intermediaries (e.g., brokers and wholesalers);
- prospective trade customers;
- consumers (and user-groups if any);
- business partners: suppliers, consortium members and JV members;
- bankers, lawyers, accountants, insurers and consultants;
- investors and their advisors (brokers and analysts);

- stock exchanges if relevant;
- alumni;
- charity and philanthropic partners;
- sponsored celebrities and sports teams;
- competitors; and
- recruitment agencies and careers advisors.

(3) **The media**

- local, national, international;
- general consumer, trade and technical;
- TV, radio, print, news agencies, freelancers, online and social.

(4) **Community stakeholders**

- neighbours – business;
- neighbours – residents;
- schools, teachers and PTAs;
- hospitals, doctors;
- police, fire brigade and emergency services;
- local voluntary groups and associations; and
- religious leaders.

(5) **Political/municipal stakeholders: local**

- MPs and candidates;
- mayor;
- councillors;
- local party chairmen;
- local government departments;

- local officials, e.g., public safety officers; and
- trading standards officers.

(6) **Industry stakeholders**
- general industry associations;
- trade bodies for your own industry sector; and
- industry sector analysts and commentators.

(7) **National/international government**
- national and EU government departments;
- national safety/consumer affairs ministers;
- relevant regulatory bodies; and
- government information departments.

(8) **Key opinion formers**
- academics;
- authors;
- industry sector gurus; and
- the 'commentariat'.

(9) **NGOs, SIGs and advocacy groups**
- pressure-groups relevant to your sector/the event;
- voluntary groups: national and international;
- consumer protection organisations; and
- safety promotion organisations.

A.2. THE 'RED BOOK'

The more materials, information and procedures you can prepare in advance, the more you can concentrate on the mayhem surrounding you when a crisis strikes. This compendium is commonly referred to as 'The Red Book'. It takes the form of both a physical manual and an online reference source.

It is a good idea to keep the procedures and systems as short as possible (so that people read them) but to make the information sections as extensive as possible. The crisis comms team will need to review the Red Book's contents regularly to make sure that everything is up to date.

(1) Policies and procedures

- complete and updated list of all internal contacts, office and personal;
- standard crisis policy: who declares crisis? How? Who takes charge?
- standard crisis procedures: who does what? Who goes where?
- standard procedures for 'typical' crises, e.g., product recalls;
- lawyers' and insurers' strictures (if any);
- roles and responsibilities of crisis comms team, e.g., fact-gathering;
- diagram of the crisis information cascade;
- comprehensive stakeholder contact database; and
- comprehensive media lists.

(2) **Media information ready to complete and/or use as it stands**

- standard corporate press kits (per unit, per brand and per site);
- Fast Facts: top-line company/brand information;
- position statements on a range of potential crises;
- backgrounder on company's record in previous crises;
- general relevant information, e.g., company's product testing systems;
- statement of company's crisis policy;
- abbreviated statement of company's mission, values and vision;
- templates for first response and follow-up statements to media;
- photographs, plans, maps, diagrams, charts, tables and graphics; and
- list of links to company's own sites and relevant external sites.

(3) **Materials for use by media communicators**

- standard media enquiry response scripts;
- media enquiry log sheets (physical and online);
- summary of coverage of previous crises (by outlet); and
- quick reference spokesperson/topic list.

Note: much of this information can also be kept up to date, and made available to media and stakeholders, on a 'dark site' (usually a separate URL) or on a section of the main website's front page which is lit up when a crisis occurs. These measures take pressure off the crisis communications team by providing background and real-time information to media without emails or phone calls.

A.3. FURTHER RESOURCES

There are four really good books on crisis communications which I would recommend to anyone who wants to acquire mastery of this intricate practice area. Two from the UK, two from the US.

Michael Bland, *Communicating Out of a Crisis*, published by Macmillan in 1998.

Michael Register and Judy Larkin, *Risk Issues and Crisis Management*, published by Kogan Page in 2008.

Kathleen Fearn-Banks, *Crisis Communications – A Casebook Approach*, published by Lawrence Erlbaum Associates in 2010.

Steven Fink, *Crisis Communications – The Definitive Guide*, published by McGraw Hill in 2013.

There are numerous websites and blogs devoted wholly or partly to crisis communications, many written by practising PR people or published by consultancies.

You can get hold of crisis communications case-studies from several sources including the Social Science Research Network and the *Harvard Business Review*. *HBR* provides several items free, then you have to subscribe.

My top recommendation is *The Holmes Report*. Every year, Paul Holmes' team pick their 10 or 12 best examples of crisis communications episodes from the previous year, giving an account of what happened, their own opinion and the opinions of leading PR experts on how communications were handled and how they could have been improved.

For verifying posts, tweets and other online items which may trigger a crisis, there is an excellent online resource: *The Verification Handbook*, edited by Craig Silverman and Rita Tsubaki. It is intended for investigative journalists but it is equally useful for us.

PRCA Training offers a range of one-day workshops, webinars and bespoke training sessions on crisis communications management. One of the PRCA's partners, Polpeo, offers social media crisis simulations which receive glowing reports from participants. If you want to train spokespeople for crisis situations (and I hope you will), there are numerous individuals and organisations who can provide realistic media training – valuable for CEOs who are used to gentle treatment from the media but need to be prepared for the very different attitude they are likely to encounter when their company is in the throes of a crisis.

A.4. READER ENQUIRIES

PRCA Training courses provide a follow-up service for people who want to ask the presenter questions after the workshop or webinar.

This book is the same. Readers are invited to contact the author with questions or to discuss any aspect of the content.

The author's address is adrianwheelerpr@gmail.com

REFERENCES

Ahmed, K. (2015). BBC business editor Kamal Ahmed: Volkswagen's problem is it 'doesn't speak human'. *PRWeek*, September 25, 2015. Retrieved from https://www.prweek.com/article/1365918/bbc-business-editor-kamal-ahmed-volkswagens-problem-doesnt-speak-human

Alan, C. (2007). In parting shot, Blair calls press a 'Feral Beast'. *New York Times*, June 12, 2007. Retrieved from https://www.nytimes.com/2007/06/12/world/europe/12cnd-blair.html

BBC.com. (2010). GM recalls 1.3m cars over power steering fault. BBC.com, March 2, 2010. Retrieved from http://news.bbc.co.uk/1/hi/business/8544989.stm

BBC.com. (2015). Corfu gas deaths: Thomas Cook has 'nothing to apologise for'. BBC.com, May 7, 2015. Retrieved from https://www.bbc.co.uk/news/uk-england-leeds-32624970

Berman, J. (2014). The three essential Warren Buffett quotes to live by. *Forbes*, April 20, 2014. Retrieved from https://www.forbes.com/sites/jamesberman/2014/04/20/the-three-essential-warren-buffett-quotes-to-live-by/#5577fe366543

Blackhurst, C. (2014). Maybe it's because they're London banks, they don't pay the living wage. *The Independent*, November 8, 2014. Retrieved from https://www.independent.

co.uk/news/business/comment/maybe-its-because-theyre-london-banks-they-dont-pay-the-living-wage-9848199.html

Blair, T. (2007). Reuters speech on public life. New York Times, June 12, 2007. Retrieved from http://news.bbc.co.uk/1/hi/uk_politics/6744581.stm

Caulkin, S. (2011). Swap the management-speak for plain English. *Financial Times*, May 9, 2011. Retrieved from https://www.ft.com/content/40006faa-701c-11e0-bea7-00144feabdc0

Chapman, B. (2017). Morrisons data leak: Thousands of staff to receive payout in landmark judgment over personal details posted online. *The Independent*, December 1, 2017. Retrieved from https://www.independent.co.uk/news/business/news/morrisons-data-leak-staff-payout-details-sensitive-data-personal-online-hack-a8086521.html

ContinuityCentral.com. (2017). British Airways: Heaping a crisis on top of a disaster. ContinuityCentral.com, May 30, 2017. Retrieved from https://www.continuitycentral.com/index.php/news/business-continuity-news/2027-british-airways-heaping-a-crisis-on-top-of-a-disaster

Craven, N. (2015). Fury of Alton Towers girl who lost leg in rollercoaster horror as theme park's boss tells her: 'We've lost a lot of money'. *Daily Mail*, September 26, 2015. Retrieved from http://www.dailymail.co.uk/news/article-3250358/Alton-Towers-boss-tells-Smiler-victim-ve-lost-lot-money.html

Czarnecki, S. (2017). Timeline of a crisis: United Airlines. *PRWeek*, June 6, 2017. Retrieved from https://www.prweek.com/article/1435619/timeline-crisis-united-airlines

Davies, R. (2015). Starbucks pays UK corporation tax of £8.1m. *The Guardian*, December 15, 2015. Retrieved from https://www.theguardian.com/business/2015/dec/15/starbucks-pays-uk-corporation-tax-8-million-pounds

Dean, J. (2016). Millions of Samsung phones recalled over exploding batteries. *The Times*, September 3, 2016. Retrieved from https://www.thetimes.co.uk/article/millions-of-samsung-phones-recalled-over-exploding-batteries-hmrxdwgzt

Dezenhall, E. (2008). Controlling a political crisis. March 17, 2008. Retrieved from http://www.washingtonpost.com/wp-dyn/content/story/2008/03/17/ST2008031700974.html??noredirect=on

Hilton, A. (2017). Anthony Hilton: BA's crisis highlights dangers of cost-cutting. *Evening Standard*, June 1, 2017. Retrieved from https://www.standard.co.uk/business/anthony-hilton-ba-s-crisis-highlights-dangers-of-costcutting-a3554686.html

HistoryNet. (2007). Admiral Cunningham and HMS Illustrious in Malta during World War II. HistoryNet, April 19, 2007. Retrieved from http://www.historynet.com/admiral-cunningham-and-hms-illustrious-in-malta-during-world-war-ii.htm

Williams, R. (2013). iPhone electric shock reportedly kills Chinese bride-to-be. *Daily Telegraph*, July 15, 2013. Retrieved from https://www.telegraph.co.uk/technology/news/10180428/iPhone-electric-shock-reportedly-kills-Chinese-bride-to-be.html

Johnson, P. (1984). Public relations. *The Spectator*, March 10, 1984. Retrieved from http://archive.spectator.co.uk/article/10th-march-1984/14/public-relations

Johnston, & Woolf. (2014). Virgin Galactic will continue after fatal SpaceShipTwo crash, vows Branson. *The Guardian*, November 1, 2014. Retrieved from https://www.theguardian.com/business/2014/nov/01/branson-virgin-galactic-spaceshiptwo-crash. Accessed on August 2018.

Karabell, S. (2010). Concentric circles: Inside the world of Sir Martin Sorrell. INSEAD, March 10, 2010. Retrieved from https://knowledge.insead.edu/leadership-management/inside-the-world-of-sir-martin-sorrell-1164

Kissinger, H. (2014). *World order*. London: Penguin Books Limited.

Layne, K. (2014). Chevron rewards survivors of fracking explosion with pizza coupon. Gawker.com, February 18, 2014. Retrieved from http://gawker.com/chevron-rewards-survivors-of-fracking-explosion-with-pi-1525276797

Matousek, M. (2018). United can't avoid customer service scandals — And it's becoming the company's greatest crisis. Business Insider, March 22, 2018. Retrieved from http://uk.businessinsider.com/united-customer-service-problems-2018-3

McCutcheon, D. (2015). How General Electric CEO Jack Welch learned to love human resources. *Financial Post*, June 10, 2015. Retrieved from https://business.financialpost.com/executive/c-suite/how-general-electric-ceo-jack-welch-learned-to-love-human-resources

Media First. (2014). Kegworth plane crash 25 years on: A media first analysis. Media First, January 8, 2014. Retrieved from https://www.mediafirst.co.uk/our-thinking/kegworth-plane-crash-25-years-on-a-media-first-analysis/

Museum of Public Relations. (2015). The first press release. The Museum of Public Relations, November 2, 2015. Retrieved from http://www.prmuseum.org/blog/2015/11/2/the-first-press-release

O'Neill, S. (2018). Oxfam chief Mark Goldring quits over Haiti sex scandal. *The Times*, May 17, 2018. Retrieved from https://www.thetimes.co.uk/article/oxfam-chief-mark-goldring-quits-over-haiti-sex-scandal-9dbtwtxcx

Parloff, R. (2018). How VW paid $25 billion for 'dieselgate' — And got off easy. *Fortune*, February 6, 2018. Retrieved from http://fortune.com/2018/02/06/volkswagen-vw-emissions-scandal-penalties/

Rankin, J. (2016). Flamanville: France's beleaguered forerunner to Hinkley Point C. *The Guardian*, July 27, 2016. Retrieved from https://www.theguardian.com/environment/2016/jul/27/flamanville-france-edf-nuclear-reactor-hinkley-point-c

Rehak, J., & *International Herald Tribune*. (2002). Tylenol made a hero of Johnson & Johnson: The recall that started them all. *International Herald Tribune*, March 23, 2002. Retrieved from https://www.nytimes.com/2002/03/23/your-money/tylenol-made-a-hero-of-johnson-johnson-the-recall-that-started.html

Reuters Staff. (2009). Tiger Woods scandal cost shareholders up to $12 billion. *Reuters*, December 29, 2009. Retrieved from https://www.reuters.com/article/us-golf-woods-shareholders/tiger-woods-scandal-cost-shareholders-up-to-12-billion-idUSTRE5BS38I20091229

Sayle, M. (2012). @indyvoices. Retrieved from https://www.telegraph.co.uk/news/obituaries/culture-obituaries/books-obituaries/8016790/Murray-Sayle.html.

Schlosser, E. (2013). *Command and control*. London: Penguin Press.

Scott, E. (2018). Starbucks incident is a reminder that 'liberal' companies with 'woke' leaders also have racism issues. *The Washington Post*, April 18, 2018. Retrieved from https://www.washingtonpost.com/news/the-fix/wp/2018/04/18/starbucks-incident-is-a-reminder-that-liberal-companies-with-woke-leaders-also-have-racism-issues/?utm_term=.2b8e09f4b686. Accessed on August 2018.

Silverman, C. (2018). Verification handbook. May 13, 2018. Retrieved from http://verificationhandbook.com/

Sobot, R., & Greatrex, C. (2016). Female caretaker mauled to death by Bengal tiger in Benidorm zoo. *Daily Mirror*, July 2, 2016. Retrieved from https://www.mirror.co.uk/news/world-news/female-zoo-worker-mauled-death-8335727

Spurgeon, C. (1859). Gems from Spurgeon. Retrieved from https://www.azquotes.com/quote/280417

Statt, N. (2017). Uber's new CEO tells employees there is 'high cost to a bad reputation' after London ban. *The Verge*, September 22, 2017. Retrieved from https://www.theverge.com/2017/9/22/16352666/uber-ceo-dara-khosrowshahi-london-ban-statement-reputation

Taleb, N. N. (2012). *Antifragile*. London: Penguin Books.

The Economist. (2009). Triple bottom line. *The Economist*, November 17, 2009. Retrieved from https://www.economist.com/news/2009/11/17/triple-bottom-line

The Telegraph. (2010). Murray Sayle. *The Guardian*, September 21, 2010. Retrieved from https://www.telegraph.co.uk/news/obituaries/culture-obituaries/books-obituaries/8016790/Murray-Sayle.html

Warner, J. (2010). BP oil disaster: Banks should learn a thing or two in handling a crisis. *Daily Tele*graph, April 26, 2010. Retrieved from https://www.telegraph.co.uk/finance/comment/jeremy-warner/7636531/BP-oil-disaster-banks-should-learn-a-thing-or-two-in-handling-a-crisis.html

Washington Post. (2008). Retrieved from Washingtonpost.com. Accessed on March 17, 2008.

Weyer, M. V. (2017). BA's disaster plan failed as soon as the smoke started coming out of its servers. *The Economist*, June 3, 2017. Retrieved from https://www.spectator.co.uk/2017/06/bas-disaster-plan-failed-as-soon-as-the-smoke-started-coming-out-of-its-servers/

INDEX